2nd Edition!

THE ENERGY OF EMOTION

By Award-Winning Author
Donna Scott-Nusrala

**3 Steps to Getting
Happy, Healthy and Abundant
with
Positive
Emotional
Programming**

Contact author at:

AMO Publishing LLC
P.O. BOX 10
Gates Mills, OH 44040
donna@amopublishing.com
www.AMOpublishing.com

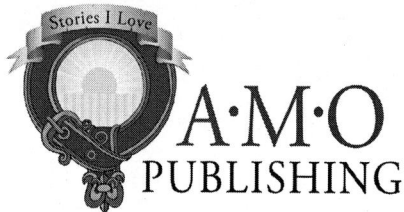

Library of Congress Control Number:
2013923097

ISBN 978-0-9840227-4-8

Printed in U.S.A.

Dedication

To my higher power
For creating the circumstances
That brought this information to me.
I am truly blessed.

Table of Contents

Foreword ix
Introduction xi

Chapter 1   Everything Is Energy 1
Chapter 2   Oxygenating the Body 3
Chapter 3   Oxygen and pH Levels. 6
Chapter 4   Non-GMO Organic Foods, HFCS,
             MSG, and Probiotics 8
Chapter 5   Just Breathe 10
Chapter 6   The Conscious, Subconscious, and The Sixth Sense 12
Chapter 7   A Thought Is a Thing. 15
Chapter 8   Frequency and Resonance 17
Chapter 9   The Power of Words. 19
Chapter 10   The Law of Attraction 22
Chapter 11   Our Transmitter and Our *Emoter* 25
Chapter 12   Mind, Body, and Soul. 28
Chapter 13   Prayer, Focused Thought, and Belief 30
Chapter 14   Resistance, Negative Emotional Programs,
             and Target Emotions 33
Chapter 15   Lack 37
Chapter 16   I Just Don't Get It! 40
Chapter 17   Energy of Emotion and The Bible Analogy 43
Chapter 18   More Analogies. 45
Chapter 19   Programs Are Generational Like Chain Links. 47
Chapter 20   **Step 1:** Finding the Negative Emotion or Target. 50
Chapter 21   Circuits and EFT 54
Chapter 22   The Path to Freedom 57

Chapter 23   **Step 2:** The Process for Releasing Negative
            Emotional Attachments. 59
Chapter 24   Feeling a Shift and PEP 63
Chapter 25   What Now?. 65
Chapter 26   You Were Born That Way 67
Chapter 27   **Step 3:** Reprogramming with PEP, Positive
            Emotional Programming. 69
Chapter 28   Positive Emotional Programming (PEP) 70

Afterword 74

Appendix
    Negative Emotional Programs. 76
    Negative Emotional Release Statements 78
    Positive Emotional Programs. 81
    Positive Emotional Programming Statements. 83
    My Goal 85
    Define Your Goal. 87
    Re-Minders 89
    Gratitude List. 90
    Dowsing or Divining. 92
    Finding Negative Emotional Programs With a Pendulum 94

Glossary. 97
Suggested Reading 105
References and Special Thanks. 107

"Donna was highly recommended by our friends as a very effective energy coach. Initially, I was skeptical that anyone could have results by spending an hour on the phone. After a couple of phone sessions, I was completely convinced that Donna's technique is effective and powerful. The greatest relief from physical pain I experienced was when I had a severe pain in my neck, shoulder, and arm. I was in so much pain that I couldn't work, cook, or drive. I didn't want to take drugs or painkillers. After the first session, I felt significantly better, and by the end of the fourth phone session, my pain was gone without taking a single pharmaceutical drug.

"I believe that Donna's technique works for two reasons. One, she is constantly learning new methods and improving her technique, and two, she addresses the emotions and feelings that are at the root of any physical pain/illness. She also empowered me by teaching me a simple tapping technique that I can use at home to feel better. My husband and I have reached out to her for help for more than two years and have been happy with the results every time. I cannot thank Donna enough, not only for her ability, but also for being such a great friend and mentor."

—MT

"The process of acknowledging, confronting, and allowing and then releasing points of energy stuck in my body were intriguing to me when Donna first worked with me. My experiences have been incredible and have truly changed my life in ways that could be categorized as miraculous.

"I am like most of you, always looking for a 'quick fix' to anger, pain, and circumstances that really frustrate daily life. These processes can and do help me acknowledge, confront, and then handle situations and life upsets. I have had so very many wins working with Donna, as well as applying the techniques described in this book as self-help, that I can say I know the method in this book works!

"I believe we are energetic beings who live in a field of magnetic and electrical energy that is in motion all the time. But just like a stream of water, sometimes the flow gets diverted, slowed, or stopped. These simple steps help locate and release the slowed or stuck energy and release the negative charge creating the interference.

"I find that I must be willing and ready to see that I created the pain, frustration, or unpleasant life circumstance before it will release. But once I do, the speed at which the energetic field can and will reset to peace and harmony is amazing.

"Just try it yourself and you may find a new world of self-help you could only have dreamed of in the past."

—DJK

"I believe that Donna has a God-given gift for opening minds and clearing bodies of unhealthy emotions, which she unselfishly shares with others. Donna has awakened me to a relatively stress-free dimension, a sixth sense, hitherto unknown by me. She has provided me with tools to help me deal with pain, stress, fear, and their physical manifestations in my body. I am experiencing a new freedom from emotional baggage and energy blockages. I am able to view my creator and life in a whole new light. My intimacy with God has expanded. I am deeply grateful to Donna."

—SJS

Foreword

It started in 2003. I had been away from teaching for three years and was busy raising three boys. After teaching middle school math and science for years, I found myself on the library floor reading picture books and assessing them for educational value. It occurred to me that the books my boys and I liked best were the ones that appealed to our senses and left us with something to ponder. The books with spoon-fed information or simple stories left us empty. I became passionate about expanding thought and encouraging creativity by appealing to the senses. That evolved into writing children's books.

I created my first book called *The Metric Family*. My intention was to show kids a simple correlation between metric units. It was designed to appeal to the imagination through the five senses. I believed that using imagination to communicate with the senses would help the reader easily assimilate the information. It worked like magic in the classroom. It was apparent that students could exchange units with little effort. It had a niche; there was nothing like it.

After countless rejection letters, writing workshops, and dwindling dreams, I decided to self-publish. Determined to make writing a career, I set out to a math teacher's conference in Boston. When my book was well received, I gained the confidence I needed to keep moving forward. I never could have predicted the journey that started with a desire to write kid's books appealing to the senses would prompt me to write a book about releasing negative emotional programs. Who knows what's next?

What follows is what I understand about what I have termed **Positive Emotional Programming (PEP)**. There is so much more I don't know, and my research continues every day.

The premise for writing this book is that diseases and dysfunctions are often the result of low oxygen levels and negative emotional energy. Everything is a form of energy. Energy is supposed to flow freely through things and through us. Disease and dysfunction are energy that is not flowing freely through the body or mind. An oxygenated body and a positive mind create the free flow of energy.

We have a conscious mind, a subconscious mind, and a physical body. The subconscious mind is the emotional mind. It does not have a language. It communicates with emotion or what many call our "sixth sense". The conscious mind is the rational mind. It communicates through our five senses. Our physical body uses our senses to express the emotions of the mind.

Our emotions define our lives. I learned that emotions can actually get trapped in our mind and manifest symptoms in the body. Each emotion vibrates on a specific energetic frequency.

My technique called **PEP** identifies a negative emotional program in the subconscious and translates it into words. Once identified and then translated, the trapped negative emotional program can be released with a form of acupressure called EFT. After releasing the negative program, the subconscious mind can be reprogrammed to a positive emotion using affirmations, spaced repetition, and EFT.

The result opens the flow of positive energy. I believe that **Positive Emotional Programming** can change lives.

For the past five years, I have applied my understanding of science to what I have studied about quantum physics or the study of energy in its simplest (purest, subatomic) form. The following pages are the culmination of thousands of hours of reading, seminars, and experimentation. It is an introduction to what I learned and what I believe and understand about energy. There is much more to learn.

This book is designed as a guide for those who are ready to release unwanted negative emotional programs. It is unconventional. An open mind is the only way to understand it. Many people would prefer to keep their poor health and negative mind, and stay in their current condition. I believe that those people are not ready for **PEP**. It takes some effort, commitment, and willingness to do this, but the benefits are life-changing.

Introduction

I have had success coaching people to release emotional resistances linked to symptoms of severe body pain like fibromyalgia, sciatica, migraine, chronic pain anywhere, fears, fear of flying, fear of criticism, depression, abuse, allergies, food allergies, panic, sadness, grief, memory loss, anxiety, loss of job, lack of money, fear of failure, panic, postsurgical pain and discomfort, PMS, knee pain, hip pain, hot flashes, insomnia, grief, addiction, arthritis, digestive disorders, relationship upsets, and symptoms like those of diabetes and many other programs.

I grant copy permission of the appendix to those with the intention of releasing emotional programs and reprogramming themselves, helping others, or for classroom purposes. You can use this book on your own or with a partner.

Disclaimer

*Not everyone who tried **Positive Emotional Programming (PEP)** could say that their symptoms were completely released, but most subjects felt a shift in their energy and many attributed changes in their lives as a result. This book is an opinion based on research. It is in no way meant to cure illness or replace health care from professionals. The author of this book accepts no responsibility or liability whatsoever for the use or misuse of the information herein. The reader knowingly assumes all risks including any adverse effects, loss or damage of any nature, or claims wherein association with this book or any suggested readings. By continuing to read this book, you are agreeing to this disclaimer and accept full responsibility for any and all risks associated with reading it and hold the author harmless.*

CHAPTER 1

Everything Is Energy

Everything is energy. Everything in the universe vibrates on frequencies. All things have an energetic frequency just like radio and television frequencies. Trees, animals, buildings, and we are made out of energy. Every **thing** we see, hear, touch, smell, taste, and feel is made of different combinations of masses of energy. Science has taught us that everything is made of very small particles called atoms. Atoms are made of smaller pieces called protons, neutrons, and electrons. The parts of protons, neutrons, and electrons are called quarks and leptons, but ultimately **everything** is energy in its simplest form.

Humans process energy with the five senses. We use our body to taste, touch, smell, hear, and see things in our environment. Open-minded thinkers are rediscovering a sixth sense—the sense of thought or intention caused by the **energy of emotion.** Intention and emotion are now known to be a measurable and moveable thing made of energy. One tool that measures emotion is a lie detector or polygraph machine. It measures changes in the flow of energy through the body because of a variation in emotion.

Energy is meant to flow freely through us and through things. I have learned that it is possible for masses of energy to get trapped in us. Our emotions can create congestion, blockages, resistance, interference, or just a feeling of being stuck. Emotions can influence our body, mind, and actions. Emotions, thoughts, and intentions are closely linked, but they are different frequencies.

Just like television or radio **frequencies,** we use our emotions to send **broadcasts** to the universe with our brain. Frequencies are the rate of oscillations or vibrations. We are like **electromagnets.** Just as a television picks up a signal and then transmits it to the screen, the frequencies we broadcast are picked up by matching magnetic frequencies then returned to us. People around us pick up our frequencies and respond to them with their emotions and send their own frequencies. We create our daily lives by these broadcasts. The people, circumstances, and events in our lives are simply an electromagnetic attraction based on our emotions.

If we are broadcasting clear, uninterrupted frequencies, they are matched and returned to us, but when a blockage occurs in the transmission, disease or dysfunction can manifest. These blockages seem to start in our mind. If they are not released, they manifest symptoms in the body. Some blockages are beliefs, while others are feelings. Blockages slow down the flow of energy through the body and decrease the flow of oxygen. A body that is not properly oxygenated will stop or slow down the broadcasts.

The goal of **Positive Emotional Programming** (PEP) is to release blockages and allow the natural flow of energy through the body and mind, and to the universe in an open and free-flowing circuit. When we broadcast negative thoughts and feelings, we create stoppages in the flow of energy, and we feel bad. If we create a habit of it, we begin to manifest symptoms of disease and dysfunction. Disease and dysfunction is our body's way of telling us we are not broadcasting positive frequencies. Getting our minds to shift from negative to positive emotional energy creates an open flow of energy through us, and we begin to rebalance.

CHAPTER 2

◦⌒ℰ⌒⌐⌒◦

Oxygenating the Body

Think of a car. It requires good fuel and maintenance to run properly. The better we care for it, the more mileage we will get out of it. Our body works the same way. Our fuel is oxygen. **Oxygen** is life.

When we place stress on our body, it demands more oxygen. That is also why we pant when we exercise or feel stress. Negative emotional energy slows down the flow of oxygen to the body. Oxygenating the body is critical to a healthy body and mind.

If we focus on foods that contain oxygen and give off oxygen in a chemical reaction such as vitamins and minerals, our body will give us more mileage and optimal function.

The movement toward raw and vegetative diets is a direct result of the knowledge that these foods oxygenate the body. We spend a lot of time and money looking for answers to health concerns. There is a barrage of information about various nutrient supplements, vitamins, and minerals. It is overwhelming and intimidating to filter all of the information coming to us in relation to getting a healthy body.

I am NOT a doctor or an expert, but based on what I have discovered, researched, read, and experienced, a healthy body comes from oxygenating it. Eating close to nature provides the best supply of oxygen. The process of juicing vegetables and fruits is effective because, when we chop them up, we are breaking the cell wall and allowing oxygen to escape. When we drink a fresh juice drink, we take in the oxygen atoms. Juicing reduces the need for the body to break down the vegetables. Drinking juice as soon as it is broken down provides the most benefit. If it sits too long, the oxygen escapes into the atmosphere, and the juice loses oxygen. Some say that they feel a "high" when they drink a fresh juice drink. It is the result of the high levels of oxygen going right into the bloodstream. Drinking juice regularly helps to open up the flow of energy through the body. When we chew our food, our teeth grind up and break the food's cell wall so the oxygen is released. When we scarf down our food, the stomach is given the responsibility of breaking it down. The stomach is doing the job the teeth were meant to do. (Cows chew and re-chew grass to maximize their oxygen intake—one reason that grass-fed beef is a healthier choice.)

Not only are the obvious foods like fruits and vegetables oxygenating to the body, but some foods create an oxygenating chemical reaction. Iron is a mineral that produces oxygen. When we eat foods high in iron, we oxygenate the body. Salt such as Himalayan Pink Salt or clean sea salt are high in minerals needed to create the chemical reaction of oxygenating the body. When hospitalized, we receive IV fluids that often include a salt/mineral magnesium solution. Magnesium helps oxygenate and hydrate the body. Magnesium is found in the soil and in pure sea or Himalayan Pink salt. Pure organic teas and certain herb combinations oxygenate the body in a chemical reaction.

Foods in nature that trap oxygen atoms keep them trapped until the food is digested. Some of these foods include honey and pure maple syrup. Unfiltered, raw honey contains pollen from the plant. Unfiltered honey is better than clear honey because the pollen is trapped in the fluid, and the oxygen is trapped in the pollen. Manuka honey is harvested from bees that pollinate the Manuka bush. The Manuka plant is known for its antiseptic properties and Tea Tree Oil. An antiseptic has high levels of oxygen and breaks down fungus and bacteria. Killing unwanted fungus and bacteria in the body opens the flow of energy.

In the oxygen cycle, plants give off oxygen and animals breathe and process it. Then, animals give off carbon dioxide and plants process it. We need plants because we can't live without oxygen. Plants need us because they cannot live without carbon dioxide. Trees give off oxygen, and pure maple syrup is a gift from the maple tree. Maple syrup contains trapped oxygen. The fluid is broken down in the stomach, and the oxygen is released. The benefits of pure maple syrup are now being revealed.

When eating meat, consider what the animal was fed. Animals fed diets high in oxygen develop flesh high in vitamins and minerals that oxygenate our bodies. Animals that graze on grass are breaking the cell walls as they chew and taking in the oxygen. Animals that eat genetically modified grain are not oxygenating their bodies and are not as healthy.

"Life is in the blood."

—The Bible

▐▐ CONSIDER THESE OXYGENATING FOODS

Non-GMO

Organic

Pasture-raised

Chemical-free

All fresh organic fruits and vegetables, especially greens and cruciferous vegetables

Sprouting plants such as broccoli, beans, brown rice, amaranth, quinoa, millet, buckwheat, garbanzo, lentil, adzuki bean, flax seed, sunflower seen, pumpkin, chia, and sesame

Raw honey

Maple syrup

Organic, pasture-raised eggs

Grass-fed meat

Free-range animals

Organic teas

Organic herbs

Organic beans are high in oxygenating iron

Wild fish

Himalayan pink salt

Organic seeds; raw, shelled, hemp seeds; fresh ground flax seeds; chia seeds; and pumpkin seeds

Kefir

Organic yogurt

CHAPTER 3

Oxygen and pH Levels

There is a lot attention given to pH and acid in the body. The **pH** of any solution is the measure of its hydrogen-ion concentration. It is known that an acidic body is an environment for disease. Stress and illness lowers the level of oxygen in the body, creating an acidic body. Oxygen rebalances the body and changes the pH level. The higher the pH reading, the more alkaline and oxygen-rich the body is. The lower the pH reading, the more acidic and oxygen-deprived the body is. The pH range is from 0 to 14, with **7.0** being neutral. Ideally, the human body should have a pH of about 7.4, which is slightly alkaline.

It is interesting to know that baking soda can help balance pH. A molecule of baking soda contains three atoms of oxygen. Baking soda is oxygenating to the body. In a chemical reaction with water, oxygen is released. Drinking a glass of water with baking soda helps oxygenate the body and balance pH. It is not the same when we bake with baking soda. The oxygen is released into the air, and the benefit is diminished in cooking. Eating foods that oxygenate the body will balance the pH.

I would also like to share one of my favorite experiments I did with Oxiclean, the cleaning product. I had been researching the benefits of oxygen, oxygenation, and oxidation. I wanted to see how Oxiclean worked to remove stains because I had the idea that over-oxygenating mold or fungus would destroy it at the cellular level. I tried liquid Oxiclean in my shower with the hope of removing the mold that could not be removed with any other product that I tested. At first I applied liquid Oxiclean and scrubbed, but I was not impressed. Nothing came off.

After my research about energy, frequency, vibration, oxygenation, and oxidation, I decided to try to over-oxygenate the mold by making a paste out of the powdered form of Oxiclean, then immediately putting it on the mold. I realized that I needed to apply it quickly after mixed with water because the chemical reaction occurred immediately and that was when the most oxygen was released. The goal was to suffocate the mold with too much oxygen just as people suffocate if they have too much carbon dioxide. It had to be done right away before the oxygen escaped into the air.

What happened amazed me. I noticed as I stood near it there was almost a "breeze" coming from it. Could that have been the release of oxygen into the air? The next day, I washed off the Oxiclean and found the mold had disappeared. The liquid form of Oxiclean didn't work and didn't give off the "breeze" because it had already gone through the chemical reaction when mixed with water in the bottle. The oxygen had already been released for the most part. The powdered form worked because the reaction was immediate, and the high level of oxygen killed the fungus and mold. That experiment validated my thought—just as a balloon explodes with too much air, over-oxygenation can kill plants and mold. Could it be concluded that too much carbon dioxide makes people ill or worse? People are killing themselves with oxygen deprivation and too much CO_2, and they don't even realize it.

New information about hydrogen peroxide, H_2O_2 and ozone, O_3 therapy, and oxygenating the body is worth your attention.

CHAPTER 4

Non-GMO Organic Foods, HFCS, MSG, and Probiotics

While at the grocer, I overheard a clerk tell an elderly man the benefits of buying organic, non-GMO foods and removing as much high fructose corn syrup from his diet as he could. The man replied, "I am way too old and sick to worry about that." It made me sad to think that he was dismissing the very thing that could make him feel better because of a mindset that organic food is a waste of money. I believe that anyone who takes the journey to understand the benefits of eating clean, non-GMO food can respond to the debate of cost versus health benefit. There is so much research now about how organic food is superior and how high fructose corn syrup is detrimental to health. Organic foods offer more nutrition, oxygen, vitamins, and minerals.

Genetically modified foods are those produced by the big food companies. They are resistant to disease and yield much higher quantities. GMO foods and food sprayed with Roundup and other pesticides kill the healthy flora in the gut and create chemical build up in the body that stops the flow of energy. Unfortunately, the human body does not recognize these genetically engineered foods, and ultimately those foods do not oxygenate the body like their original varieties. Our society is sick and grossly overweight because we are eating things that our body cannot process or use to create oxygen. Organic foods are those that are grown and created the way in which nature intended. Foods sprayed with pesticides and animals given growth hormones are a recipe for illness, disease, and blockages in the energy flow. These things are not recognized or processed by the body as food.

Processed foods that have sugar substitutes, high fructose corn syrup, corn sugar, butter substitutes, and MSG products slow down the free flow of energy and even create blockages. The body does not recognize any of these things as foods that can be digested or metabolized. They do not oxygenate the body. Energy flow diminishes with these foods.

Consider the probiotic and/or the digestive enzyme movement. People are learning that they are depleted of necessary digestive ingredients. It is said that you are only as healthy as your gut. With all of the processed and genetically modified food, drugs, and processed food, the American gut is a cesspool. The gut is supposed to be an ecosystem of its own. It contains flora and fauna that uses oxygen for processing food. When it is fed antibiotics, the flora and fauna are wiped out, which leaves the gut vulnerable to all sorts of ailments. The oxygen levels become depleted, and body functions slow down. Energy slows down and cannot flow freely. Processed foods do not support a healthy gut.

Candida is a fungus that is a by-product of an unhealthy gut. Sugar feeds Candida, and it grows rampant in the body causing a host of ailments from digestive disorders to skin issues and more. A red glow in the face or a rash could be a signs of a Candida overgrowth. Oxygenating helps rebalance the gut and keep Candida at bay. Taking a probiotic regularly can help balance the flora and fauna of the gut and create an oxygenating environment to help with healthy digestion.

CHAPTER 5

⌑

Just Breathe

It sounds so simple, but just the act of deep breathing is oxygenating to the body. That is why health professionals say that going for a walk outside is good for our health. Meditation and deliberate breathing is oxygenating and calming too. It is critical to move the body to keep the flow of energy going. Stagnation slows energy down. We can get creative about how to increase our air intake. Energy needs to be in motion. The more we can consciously help that happen, the better we improve the flow of energy.

Create a habit of sitting up straight and pulling in some deep breaths while driving or at your desk. It is amazing how much more alert we can feel. Just the act of sitting up straight and breathing helps oxygenate the body. Being consciously aware of our breathing makes us realize that we often are breathing very shallow or even holding our breath at times. We hold our breath in response to stress.

Another great way to add oxygen is to have plants in our homes. They are nature's air purifiers, adding clean oxygen while clearing out the carbon dioxide. Exercising and dancing are also a good way to oxygenate and don't need to be rigorous to be beneficial.

Consider the things we put on our skin. Makeup, lotions, and creams can slow down the flow of oxygen. Our skin is our largest organ, and it is very absorbent. Anything we put on the skin gets absorbed and has an effect on the levels of oxygen. Oils, soaps, and makeups that contain chemicals and GMO ingredients clog pores. When we use lotions, shampoos, and creams, we are putting chemicals directly into our bodies. Anything that we put on the skin should be oxygenating and not slow the flow of energy through the body.

Other things to consider are the clothes we wear and the bedding we sleep in. Synthetic fibers stop the flow of oxygen through the skin. Man-made materials do not allow the body to easily take in oxygen through the skin. That is why we perspire more when we wear or sleep in fabrics that don't breathe. Wools and cottons, silks, and natural fibers allow the free flow of oxygen to our skin. Our skin needs to breathe; it is like a sponge. Organic fibers are even better because they were raised without chemicals. Some cotton fabric is sprayed with Teflon or other coatings to make it wrinkle-free. Take a look at what your clothes and bedding are sprayed with.

A healthy body that can breathe and process oxygen in cooperation with an open, positive mind is the right combination. We need to do all we can to create the free flow of oxygen and move energy through us. When we do that, we can broadcast and receive the frequencies that create the life that we desire. It is just like keeping our car maintained with good oil and gasoline so that it can get us where we want to go.

CHAPTER 6

The Conscious, Subconscious, and The Sixth Sense

We function on two levels. First, there is the **conscious mind**. We interpret the world with our five senses and our conscious mind. It is how we rationalize our world. We process information with the five senses and use our brain to interpret what we see, hear, touch, smell, and taste.

The second level is the **subconscious mind**. It is how we sense the world using our emotions and feelings. Touch is not the same as feeling. Our sixth sense is our subconscious mind. It is where we feel our emotions. We cannot see, hear, taste, touch, or smell our emotions. We feel them. We process them with our heart, and then we send them out or **emote** them. Another term for emoting is **broadcasting** emotion.

We process energy in the conscious mind with our five senses. Sound is energy vibrating at a frequency we can hear. We can see sound waves that are sent through a tangible medium. Watch water vibrate and ripple when a loud sound runs through it. That is energy vibrating on sound frequencies.

Listening to music makes us feel a certain way. It actually influences our thinking. Music appeals to more than just our sense of hearing. A song is a combination of sounds on frequencies, and if we like what we hear, we begin to attach an emotion to it with our heart. If played repeatedly, we begin to resonate with the emotion that song gives us. More than that, we begin to broadcast the feeling it gives us. Did you know that we create circumstances and attract people into our lives based on broadcasts?

We can see and feel frequencies with our body's sensory receptors. The light from the sun has warm and bright frequencies that we can see with our eyes and sense with our skin. We feel light from the sun in invisible waves of radiation, and we respond to it with our senses. Light energy is measured on a scale called the visible spectrum. Each color of light **vibrates** at a measurable frequency. A vibration is a rate of oscillation or back-and-forth movement. We can only interpret limited frequencies with our five senses. We cannot process energy such as microwaves, gamma rays, and many others with our five senses, but they are there.

Smells are just masses of energy that our noses can sense. Popcorn has a strong smell. It has a unique frequency. When our sense of smell picks it up, we resonate with the frequency of fresh popped popcorn. Our sense of smell and taste begin to harmonize with that frequency. When that happens, we cannot resist having it. It is almost hypnotic. I am guessing you can almost smell it as you read these words.

There are things that stop or slow down our subconscious emotional broadcasts. Anything that we put in our body has mass and can create stoppages. Some things slow down the flow of energy and affect our broadcasts. Other things can open the flow, speed up oscillation, and raise our vibration. Every type of food or drug is a form of energy. Each one vibrates on a different frequency. Foods and drugs can affect, influence, or impair our broadcasts. The more oxygenated our body is, the clearer it is, and therefore the broadcast is faster and clearer. We can also slow down, stop, or change the direction of energy through us with our thoughts because a thought is a thing that has mass. Negative thoughts are slow, heavy, and dense energy. We can actually feel the dense negative thought energy in our bodies. Positive thoughts are light, faster energy. We feel light when we broadcast positive emotions.

When we repeat experiences over and over, we are actually doing a form of programming through our senses. **Programs** are frequencies embedded in our subconscious mind. Just like the grooves of a record or CD, we embed programs in our subconscious. That is how we create memories. We have the ability to accept or reject programs. Most people don't know that. We subconsciously choose to remember things. Things that appeal to our senses are embedded more easily because they are programmed both consciously and subconsciously. We can also consciously choose to forget things and delete them from our memory. Memories are often linked to our sixth sense or our emotions. We remember those things that have an emotional attachment. Think of the traumas that are stuck in your mind.

When we accept a program, we harmonize with it; we create a **sympathetic resonance** to it. Sympathetic resonance is a harmonic phenomenon wherein a vibratory body responds to a like frequency. In other words, we subconsciously agree to be on the same frequency. We attach an emotion to it and then create circumstances, situations, and events from that emotional frequency. It becomes a part of us and actually forms mass. At that point, it is a belief and a habit. We have strong feelings about it. It is our truth.

We are like a phone tower. We broadcast emotions and receive matching circumstances to those emotions. We create our life via thousands of broadcasts every day.

What is your favorite song? What feeling do you get when you hear it? When you focus on a song with strong emotion, consider what you may broadcast: love, joy, anger, resentment, victim, guilt, neediness, etc. You are broadcasting an emotion. You resonate with it. If you stay in that feeling, **you will attract similar frequencies and circumstances.**

What is your favorite movie? How does it make you feel? Love, anger, fear, terror, sadness, illness, tragedy, joy? You broadcast that frequency. You resonate with it.

CHAPTER **7**

⮂

A Thought Is a Thing

We were taught that a noun is a person, place, or thing. Applied to the study of energy, we can say that people have frequencies, places vibrate on frequencies, and each thing vibrates at a specific frequency. But the idea that a thought or emotion could be a quantifiable thing made of particle mass vibrating at specific frequencies is a bit abstract. The idea is gaining a lot of attention lately.

At this point, I would like you to stop reading and look up Dr. Masaru Emoto's YouTube videos. You can find a link on my website at *www.amopub lishing.com/bookstore/Energy-of-Emotion*. Take a look at what he discovered about words, water, thoughts, music, and sounds.

For my purpose, his experiment with words and thoughts on water crystals helps to explain how I believe emotions have mass and can be quantified.

Dr. Emoto uses a glass of water and looks at it with focused thought broadcasting the emotions linked to the word "love". Then he freezes the glass of water for 3 hours at 30 degrees below zero. He takes the water crystals and observes them under a microscope and finds them to be of a beautiful organized crystalline structure, similar to a snowflake.

He repeats the experiment focusing emotion on the word "hate". Upon observation, the structure of the crystals appears random and poor. He continues to test other emotions and finds that, when emotions with intent or prayer are focused in the water, it has a significant impact on the structure of the molecules of water. Understanding that a thought is a quantifiable and measurable thing made of particles is critical to knowing how **Positive Emotional Programming** works.

Consider this: Gold, silver, and copper are excellent conductors and amplifiers of energy. Can gold amplify intention or emotion? Gold = Money = Power. I believe that, throughout history, certain people knew that these precious metals were powerful, strong conductors that could influence emotions at the quantum level.

> *"If we are nearly 80 percent water, consider how words and emotions can have an effect on our atomic structure.*
>
> *If emotion can be attached to water, is it possible that they can attach to oxygen?*
>
> *Can we breathe in thoughts and become them?*
>
> *If we are fluid and changeable, can we influence our thoughts, our frequency, and affect our physical body?*
>
> *Can oxygen carry emotions?*
>
> *Do we BECOME our thoughts at the cellular level?*
>
> *"The molecular structure of matter changes by intention and emotion."*
>
> —Dr. Emoto

CHAPTER 8

༄ৎৣৢৢঌৢৢৢঌৢৢৢ

Frequency and Resonance

To get a picture of frequency and resonance, a basic understanding of music and electricity is helpful. When we pluck a string or sing, we create vibrations that ears pick up and interpret. The **frequency** is the number of cycles per unit or the speed. High notes have high frequencies, and low notes have low frequencies. If we like what we hear, our body will actually go into a state of **resonance** with it and vibrate at the same speed. In other words, we are agreeing, allowing, and resonating with the sounds.

When we taste a new food, our reaction could be in harmony or disharmony depending whether we like it or we don't.

If we are touched in a pleasing way, we resonate with it. If we are annoyed or offended, we do not resonate with it. Then we are not in vibrational harmony; the frequencies don't match, and we want it to stop.

We do not resonate with offensive smells. We resonate with good smells. Good smells to some are sometimes not good to others. It is all about matching frequencies. Matching frequencies is resonance.

Resonance happens in many ways. If we agree with another person in a conversation, we resonate with them. Our vibrations match, and we feel harmony. On the other hand, we feel a lack of resonance when we don't like what we hear. We are not in harmony, frequencies don't match, and we have a disagreement.

When in a place of disease or dysfunction, we are actually not harmonizing, resonating, or vibrating in congruence with ourselves, our beliefs, thoughts, and emotions. Some would say we are not aligned. Others would say that we are broadcasting negative frequencies and receiving negative frequencies. We are also stopping the natural flow of energy through our body and mind.

To me, the obvious solution to disease and dysfunction is to get the mind back into resonance with the frequencies of its intended purpose and allow the energy to flow freely through the body, increasing the flow of oxygen.

The idea that the body wants to be in resonance or alignment to be healthy is not new. Yoga, Reiki, EFT, Qi Gong, psychology, acupuncture, proper nutrition, and many other techniques have been introduced in a variety of ways with that goal in mind. People who work with chakras are balancing energy in the body and helping the mind and body resonate.

What is new for me is the discovery that a strong focus on very specific frequencies can release programs, blockages, or resistance in the mind. Restoration of harmony to the body and mind can happen upon releasing and rerouting the energy back to its intended frequency. When that happens, energy flows freely in its natural path. I am sure many techniques out there can accomplish resonance. I have found incredible and almost miraculous results using this type of releasing or rebalancing by what I call **Positive Emotional Programming**.

Could releasing disease and dysfunction be as easy as changing your mind?

An opera singer who can break a crystal glass is broadcasting the same frequency of the crystal. She has learned how to resonate with it in perfect harmony. Often it is the note of high C. When frequencies match, the glass explodes.

If everything is vibrating on a specific frequency linked to an emotion, then finding that emotion, matching the frequency, and releasing it from the mind and body should hypothetically release disease.

CHAPTER 9

The Power of Words

As a writer, I became especially aware of word usage. An editor told me, "If you want to write a picture book, you need to make every word count. Leave out the unnecessary words, and say a lot in the pictures."

Being the literal interpreter that I am, I set out to write my picture books, analyzing every word and making sure that each word had meaning for the reader to follow the story. My journey into the power of words turned into an extreme interest in the true meaning, definition, phonetic sound, tone, and actual resonance of words. What a journey that has been! I learned that words carry power, frequency, and vibration. **Words** express thought. Thought is emotion interpreted. Emotions have mass and particle flow.

I often wondered why there are "bad words". My findings led me to an amazing cognition. Words themselves are not "bad". It is the intention or emotion behind the word. The intention behind using those words is often to express emotion or to create disharmony in the recipient and influence his/her vibration. When someone swears at us, it creates confusion and interferes with our broadcasts.

"Our intentions and emotions seem to operate as highly coherent frequencies capable of changing the molecular structure of matter."
—Sayer Ji, "Biophotons: The Human Body Emits, Communicates with, and Is Made From Light," GreenMedInfo.com, June 2013.

Emotions and thoughts are expressed in words. Every word sets off a different vibration. The intention or emotion behind a word evokes a response or reaction. So when we swear and intend to send out a very focused broadcast expressing the emotion of anger or rage, we are sending and receiving a much different frequency than when we use the same word to express amazement. The emotions or intentions are focused either positively or negatively. Understanding intention is a huge step toward understanding how we create our reality and, further, **Positive Emotional Programming (PEP).**

Emotion is highly focused thought. When we are angry, we are focused. When we are thrilled, we are focused. When we are confused, we are not focused. Stress and trauma create confusion and also slow down the flow of oxygen in the body. When we are not focused, we stop, slow down, or change the direction of the flow of energy through us and influence the broadcast to the universe.

Words are a tool for expressing thought and emotion. We broadcast emotion 24/7. It happens without effort. Frequencies are always matched and returned, bringing circumstances, people, and events that match our broadcast. It is that simple. How focused are our thoughts? How much emotion have we attached to those thoughts? If our thoughts and emotions are scrambled, we are living in confusion just like static between radio stations. Our goal is to have clear, coherent thoughts so that we have clear, coherent emotional broadcasts.

If we don't understand the true meaning of words, we may use them inappropriately. When we do that, we broadcast the wrong frequency. We create and manifest the wrong things into our lives. *It is imperative that we know the meaning of words.* Always look up **misunderstood words.** Misunderstood words are words that we have not processed with our senses. Often, we attach the wrong emotion to a word if we don't understand it. More detrimental, misunderstood words cause confusion and static. When we don't understand the meaning of the words we are using, we stop the flow of energy and cause energy to divert or change direction and interfere with our intentions.

Never underestimate the power of words.

"My word is as good as gold."

—*Unknown*

"I give you my word."

—*Unknown*

"Do I make myself clear?"

—*Unknown*

Can intention, words, thoughts, or emotions change the structure of the body at the cellular level?

CHAPTER 10

⤜⟋⟍⤛

The Law of Attraction

If you have not yet been introduced to the *Law of Attraction*, I highly recommend reading *The Secret* by Rhonda Byrne, *Think and Grow Rich* by Napoleon Hill, *The Power of Positive Thinking* by Norman Vincent Peale, or *The Magic of Believing* by Claude Bristol.

Briefly oversimplified, the **Law of Attraction** describes the concept of creating what we want in life by focusing intention and visualization. If we visualize and broadcast intention with strong emotion and focus, similar frequencies in the universe match our intention and are attracted back to us because our thoughts are linked to our emotions, and emotions are magnetic.

So if we express with hope and desire "I want to be healthy" and add the emotions of joy and happiness, the circumstances, events, and situation start to line up to make it happen. Frequencies in the universe begin to match the frequency we broadcast. The speed at which it comes depends upon the clarity of the broadcast, the intensity of emotions, how often we focus, and whether it encounters interference. I have read that focusing intense emotion for one-and-a-half minutes is long enough to begin to add mass to whatever we focus upon. Focusing over and over using **spaced repetition** or doing it in spaced intervals adds mass to the thought and begins its **manifestation**. Manifestation is the creation of bringing the circumstances, events, and situations before us that match our emotional broadcasts. The more time we spend focusing thoughts with emotion, the more mass we give them. The more mass we give to our thoughts with emotion, the faster they will manifest into our reality.

If we express with hope and desire "I want to be healthy", but we are feeling doubt or fear when we broadcast the desire, we will stop it from being created. That is called **resistance**. We create more doubt or fear because doubt and fear are what we are feeling in our subconscious mind. We are diverting the energy, stopping the flow, and resisting. We get what our emotions are focused upon because emotions are magnetic. Words are only tools for expressing emotions, and sometimes our words don't match the emotion we broadcast. That is why it is critical to be keenly aware of how we are really feeling emotionally.

I believe that the trick to releasing disease with our thinking is to communicate to our subconscious mind the belief and feeling that we are well. Then matching magnetic emotional frequencies are returned to us by the *Law of Attraction*. Communicating with our subconscious mind is not difficult. It is a matter of **programming** ourselves and getting our body to resonate with our desires. Programming is done by spaced repetition through the senses or the conscious mind. Spaced repetition is the act of repeating the same information over and over again until we have created the habit like grooves in a record. We can also program ourselves through the senses by getting immersed in the desired outcome, through visualization, and by using imagination.

Sick people who are around other sick people stay sick because they are all on the same frequency of illness, creating more of it by the magnetic law of attraction. They may not have the same condition, but the frequency of illness can manifest in many ways. We all know people who love to gather together to complain about their health. They are all broadcasting *fear of illness*, and they are attracted to each other. If we hang around and listen to them long enough, we will broadcast it too. We pick up their frequency and attach an emotion to it. Then, by spaced repetition and immersion in their frequencies, we begin to manifest it in our lives by the magnetic law of attraction. A north magnet wants a south magnet.

Wealthy people hang around with other wealthy people not because they are snobs, but because they are broadcasting the frequency of wealth. By the law of attraction, they are magnetically attracting people based on the emotions that they have created about wealth. Some people were born vibrating wealth, so people, circumstances, and events that match wealth just comes to them.

The same is so for people who were born in poverty. They are subconsciously broadcasting poverty and cannot escape it until they understand that it is a subconscious program embedded in them. When they realize it is only a program that they are broadcasting, they can consciously reprogram themselves to a different reality. They program themselves by making the conscious decision to use spaced repetition and their senses. They use the conscious mind to train the subconscious mind to a different reality. Then, they release the attachment to poverty and create the reality they want.

"What you do comes back to you."

—Unknown

"You get out of it what you put into it."

—Unknown

"Do unto others as you would have them do unto you."
—The Golden Rule

"What goes around, comes around."

—Unknown

"You get back what you put out."

—Unknown

"If you hang around them long enough, you will turn out just like them."
—Unknown

"For every action, there is an equal and opposite reaction."
—Isaac Newton

"Be careful what you wish for because you just might get it all."
—Unknown

CHAPTER 11

❧

Our Transmitter and Our *Emoter*

We rely so heavily on our sense of sight that we tend to miss things that our other senses can tell us. For the most part, we have not been programmed to deliberately create our lives with intention and emotion. We tend to be reactive to life rather than proactive. In order to understand the energy of emotion, we need to understand that, not only do we function with two minds—the conscious and the subconscious mind, but also that one mind works with the brain and thought. The other mind works with the heart and feelings.

The conscious mind works with our brain. It is where we make decisions during our days. We base most of what we know to be true on the things we see, hear, touch, taste, and smell. Some people refer to the conscious mind as their radar screen. It's what they can believe is true based on what their senses tell them. The conscious mind is where we think our thoughts. We rationalize in the conscious mind using our senses. We transmit and receive logical information through the brain then process it through our senses. Our **transmitter** is the conscious mind working with the brain. The brain is where we store our memories in words that can be retrieved on demand. We use our conscious mind to solve problems based on what we know to be true, quantifiable, and tangible.

The subconscious mind works in conjunction with our heart. Our heart is the communicative device that creates our reality based on the emotions we broadcast. The subconscious mind functions on the basic instinct of flight or fight. The subconscious mind functions on the basic instinct of flight or fight; it cannot judge or make decisions. Its only job is to respond to what we broadcast from our heart with emotion. We cannot stop the subconscious mind from working. It always works just as our heart always beats effortlessly.

Our **emoter** is our heart and the subconscious mind working together. The subconscious sends and receives emotional responses to the heart and to the universe. The subconscious communicates with the higher realms or high frequencies with emotion. We broadcast emotions from the heart with the help of the subconscious mind. There are no words to broadcast, just feelings. We are always doing it. We can guide and influence our subconscious if we are in touch with our emotions. Some people are more in tune with their subconscious and their *emoter* than others. We call those people creative because they can find solutions without having tangible, touchable mass to work with. They can sense things off their radar screen.

We are emoting something at all times. Our *emoter* sends out broadcasts based on our emotions. Those broadcasts are influenced by other people's broadcasts. Our *emoter* is only as powerful as we make it. Strong, powerful *emoters* come from clear, focused people. If we are sick, weak, or emotionally out of control, our *emoter* does not work to our advantage. We must be aware of our emotions. We must guide and influence the broadcasts from our heart. The subconscious mind is magnetic. When we can take control of it, we are deliberately creating our lives, selecting what we wish to experience, and emoting what we desire.

Good and bad, positive and negative, we store our feelings in our heart. Emotions are retrieved instantly when we experience a feeling we have had before.

If we are not getting what we want from life, we need to adjust, tune into, or tune up our *emoter*. We need to find and release the negative emotions stuck in our heart that are creating the negative circumstances. **PEP** can help.

I believe that our source/God is of the highest, purest frequencies. Our emotions are broadcasted from our heart by the subconscious mind to the universe, ether, or God. Some call it prayer. We are not always consciously aware of our emotions, so we are not always consciously aware of what we are creating, broadcasting, or praying for.

Positive Emotional Programming works by interpreting the emotions of the heart through the subconscious mind, then translating those emotions into words, bringing those words into the conscious mind through the brain so we can process them with the senses. **PEP** can release and defuse the mass of energy that we attached to the emotion. After the release, the brain is trained to transmit different frequencies, and the heart is trained to broadcast different emotions.

We need to be very aware of how we feel at any given time and in every situation, because we are broadcasting those feelings. When we are aware of our broadcasts, we are living a life of purpose and intention.

God gave man free will. Free will is intention and emotion. It is the choices we make based on emotions.

"I speak to you from the heart."

"Use your head!"

CHAPTER 12

❧ ❦

Mind, Body, and Soul

Consider that we are made up of three parts. First, we have a mind, conscious and unconscious. Some say that the mind is actually a magnetic field that exists around the physical body. It sends emotions to the heart for interpretation and emotional attachment.

Then, we have a physical body. I think of it like a space suit. We use this physical body to manipulate our environment through our senses. Our body has sense receptors that give us information to process with the brain. The body also houses communication devices. One such device is our brain. It is the transmitter and receiver of information and frequencies. When we think, we transmit and receive information from our brain.

We transmit and receive emotions from our heart. The heart is the interpreter of emotions. In Einstein's equation $E=MC^2$, E represents energy. So when I use the word emoter as it relates to emotion from the heart, I think of the heart as the body's engine or motor. E-motor = energy in the motor. E = energy + Motion = emotion or energy in motion.

The heart senses situations and attaches emotion. Often, those emotions are stored in the mind from previous experiences. The mind creates a reaction or response. Then, the subconscious mind tells the conscious mind how to react or respond. The brain then sends the signals to the appropriate parts of the body. The brain receives the communication and sends it to the heart. Based on the emotion it triggers, the heart communicates with the brain and gives the command to our body to move or speak in response to the emotion broadcasted. When we live a life by thoughtful intention and keen awareness of our emotions, we are being proactive. Most people react to what happens to them rather than creating the life they want. We need to understand that we are creating our lives by magnetic emotional attractions.

"Twinkle, twinkle, little star, what you say is what you are."

—*Unknown*

"You spot, you got it."

—*Unknown*

"I Am That I Am."

—*Exodus 3:14; The Bible*

"If you think you can or if you think you can't, either way you are right. It is the thinking that make it so."

—*Henry Ford*

"God helps those who help themselves."

—*Ancient Greek proverb*

Are we attracted to people because we are matching their frequency?

When we are in love, are we just matching frequencies with intense emotion?

"It takes one to know one."

—*Unknown*

CHAPTER **13**

❧

Prayer, Focused Thought, and Belief

Somewhere in my religious education, I came across the idea that people needed to be taught how to pray. At one point, I thought it was ridiculous. Anyone should be able to communicate with his/her higher power without instruction, I thought.

Now I realize there is truth in learning how to pray. **Prayer** is focused thought mixed with emotion. **Focused thought** is intention. When we pray, we focus on what we want. Prayer with intention and emotion works well with the *Law of Attraction*. Our brains transmit thoughts, and our hearts broadcast the emotion linked to the desire. Then, by the law of attraction, we receive circumstances, events, and situations that match the frequency of our emotions.

When several people gather together and pray, the frequency intensifies because each person adds another brain or, transmitter/receiver. The effect is actually multiplied. Napoleon Hill, author of several success books, refers to this as a "mastermind". Answered prayers can be explained by the idea that words plus focused thought and emotion send out a frequency to God/source/universe. Circumstances, events, and situations that match the frequency of the prayer are picked up and returned by magnetic attraction.

It is the *Law of Attraction* in action. The frequency that is matched is the frequency of the emotion being broadcast. Some people say, "God answers my prayers." In fact, he does. Mastering the art of prayer is congruent with focusing thought with clarity, intention, and emotion.

If we pray when feeling fear, then fear is the frequency that will be matched and returned. If the broadcast is of faith, then faith is what will be matched and returned. I believe that if everything is energy, God is energy, God is everywhere, and energy is everywhere. I believe that God/source is energy at its highest, purest, strongest, fastest form, and we can communicate with emotion and intention.

Thinking and speaking is a form of creating. If a thought is a thing, and we create frequencies by our thoughts, imagine how we create our life's experiences with our emotions and intentions.

When we speak, we send out words with mass on specific frequencies backed by emotion. Thoughts and emotions influence our words. Other people's words influence our thoughts. The most intense frequencies come from what we feel. We can be intentional about our emotions if we carefully filter our thoughts and words, but also sensor the influence of thoughts and words of others.

A person with a disease can try affirmations and positive talk like, "I am healthy, I am well, and I feel great", but if he is influenced by the words of others or subconsciously broadcasting, "I am afraid of being ill", then he starts to believe that he cannot get well and broadcasts and receives from that emotion.

Beliefs are embedded emotional frequencies. They are embedded in our minds by repetition and attached emotion. Many people have an embedded *fear of illness* thanks to our culture. Emotions match the frequency of fear of illness and create more of it. That is why even the most positive people are challenged when trying to pull out of a disease. It is the positive emoters, intenders, broadcasters, or those who can focus strong positive emotion away from the fear, and convince their subconscious mind to release the fear of illness and BELIEVE that they are fine. They have miraculous results. They release the resistance and take the focus off of the condition. When we focus on having an illness, we add mass to it and create more of it. When we focus on being fine, joyful, and positive, we create more of that.

Should we fight disease? Or allow it and release resistance to it? Then forget about it.

If we fight a disease, won't we just attract more of a fight because we have attached a negative emotion to it?

Should we make people aware of illness? Cancer awareness? What do you think awareness does to your emotional broadcasts? Could we create more of it with the fear and awareness of it? What would happen if we gave it no attention? What if we made people aware that their body was more healthy than ill?

Consider why prayer has been taken out of schools. Is focused thought backed by emotion and intention too empowering?

CHAPTER 14

༄ৄৢৄ

Resistance, Negative Emotional Programs, and Target Emotions

Abasic knowledge of electricity will help us recognize resistance in this context. When doing **PEP,** resistance, energetic blockages, and negative programs are used interchangeably. If we understand electricity, we can use the analogies of a break in the circuit, resistance, or redirecting current.

To create a complete circuit, energy is taken from point A to point B and back, closing the circuit. A break in the circuit means the flow is stopped. Sometimes energy is redirected. Energy is carried in an indirect route rather than from point A to B.

Positive emotions allow the free flow of energy. Negative emotions cause **resistance.** Resistance happens when the flow of energy is diverted or slowed down. Some call it a blockage or stop in the flow of energy. When it is diverted, energy is redirected to a different emotional program.

Say we broadcast the thought "I am healthy" with intention, focus, emotion, and belief that we will manifest good health. We want to create that program in our mind. We are halfway there.

Negative emotional programs stop, slow down the flow, cause resistance, or divert the frequencies so that the circuit to good health is not complete. Energy flow is naturally positive. When we think negatively, we are fighting the natural flow.

Two of the strongest negative emotional resistors are the emotions of fear and doubt. We can find out if the frequency we are intending to broadcast is being resisted by the emotions of fear or doubt. One way is to just ask ourselves. That little voice in our head is our subconscious mind. We communicate with it regularly. We know if we are being honest.

Do we doubt we can be healthy? Do we fear we are not healthy? If that is so, then we are broadcasting the emotions of fear or doubt, and we will create more of them by magnetic attraction.

I use the word "program" because it is how we create habits. Our parents, family society, TV, computers, radio, media, teachers, friends, and people in authority influence us. We actually program ourselves. At a young age, the influence is so strong and we are so impressionable that we quickly and easily resonate with our environment. There are positive programs like healthy eating, success, love, or fulfillment. We broadcast positive emotions linked to those positive emotional programs. Positive programs feel light and good.

We also broadcast negative programs like failure, fear, worry, or poverty. We attach negative emotions to those programs. Negative programs feel heavy and bad. The negative emotions we broadcast are a direct result of our environment, the people who influence us in our environment, and the emotions we attach. Programs are created by the habit of repetition. We repeat the programs familiar to us because, in many instances, that is all we know. We stay in the same environment so we can feel safe. Fear for safety is a very strong emotion. People in authority use the fear for safety to influence us. The good news is that, once we understand this, we can reprogram ourselves with **Positive Emotional Programming, PEP.**

*H*ere is an example to help you understand even better:

Refer to the **Negative Emotional Programs Chart** on pages 76-77 of this book. Focus on a situation on your mind. Then, go through the list of emotional programs on the chart. Check off the emotional programs on the chart that resonate with you.

You will know when an emotion is resonating because you may get a sickly, scared, or sad feeling when you say it aloud or think about it. You may feel a heavy or sinking feeling. You just may have a knowing. You may feel doubt. You may rationalize that everyone feels that way. Say them out loud. You may feel discomfort, pain, or tightness in your body. As you think about the emotion, you may have flashbacks in your mind to events in your life that made you feel that emotion. That is your heart's memory recalling a similar feeling.

For this example, I am going to use the feeling of "fear for my safety" as a **target emotion.** A target emotion is one that is very real to us. It almost feels like it has an electrical charge when we think about it. It evokes emotion in the mind and discomfort in the body. The target emotion has negative charge attached that we want to release.

Safety is a big issue in the United States right now. Think about the images you have seen in the media or heard from friends about the economy and unrest in the world, your town, your home, and your life. As you think about how you fear for your safety, sense if you feel some discomfort welling up in your body somewhere. Wherever you feel the discomfort is where that emotion is stuck in your body. There is an emotional charge or attachment to it. Fear is often stored in the gut, heart, or throat. Did you flashback to a time in your life when you felt this fear? Flashbacks, like recalling where you were on 9/11, are linked like a chain. If you can feel and then verbalize the emotion this way, you are using intuition.

Using a pencil and white paper, write down all of the things that come to your mind that make you fear for your safety. Writing in pencil tells the subconscious mind that these thoughts are only temporary. I was told that writing with blue pen in cursive helps the information stay in the memory. So use blue pen and cursive when writing things you want to remember, and use pencil when you want to remember temporarily. (*Hold on to the list. We will use it later.*)

In addition to using intuition, muscle testing or applied kinesiology is another method for finding which emotional programs you resonate with. You can look up muscle testing and applied kinesiology online. The premise is that a muscle weakens when a thought is not true or the circuit weakens. Muscle testing is a means of communication with the subconscious mind. It is explained on many websites. Training videos on muscle testing and applied kinesiology are available.

My preferred method of testing for resistance, programs, or diverted energy is by divining. I have found that I can read negative emotional broadcasts and translate those emotional frequencies into words. I can communicate with the subconscious mind most effectively using divining and **PEP**. It took me a good year to train myself to divine accurately. If you are interested in learning more about divining, please refer to page 92. You don't need to know it to do **PEP**.

Did you know that schools, churches, government, news, books, billboards, TV, video games, and radio shows influence you? Can you sense the emotions they create in you? They could be negatively programming you. Isn't it interesting that we even call them programs? Some are good, and some are not so good. Even your friends, family, and coworkers influence you if you let them. The more time you spend with them, the more you resonate with them and begin to broadcast similar frequencies. It can only happen if you allow it. Once you know it is happening, you can consciously choose what you allow in your subconscious mind. **Select the programs that give you the emotion you wish to broadcast and receive in your life.**

Consider the influences that video, family, church, computers, schools, advertising, and movies have on us and on our children. We create and define our day/life by the emotions we broadcast from what we see, hear, and feel because we begin to vibrate and resonate with those programs at the cellular level.

Are you addicted to the news? Think about it. How does the newscast make you feel? Could you be attracting situations that give you fear for your safety? Does the news make you feel safe?

The Chinese definition of insanity is doing the same thing over and over and expecting a different result.

"If you always do what you've always done, you will always get what you've always gotten."

—*Unknown*

"What you resist persists."

—*Carl Jung*

"Doubt can sink a ship."

—*Unknown*

"Believe and you will achieve."

—*Napoleon Hill*

"Go with the flow."

—*Unknown*

CHAPTER 15

❦

Lack

I once worked with a girl who said, "I have no clue what it is like to feel happy." That was the catalyst for my research into *programs and missing programs, or emotions and missing emotions*. I actually learned that, just like a computer, we can have programs stuck in our minds, but we can also be missing emotional programs that we never experienced in our lives before.

Throughout our timeline, we pick up emotional programs based on our surroundings because we must resonate with those programs to survive there. We define our lives by these programs, and most of us don't question them or try to change them. They become our truths.

The girl I worked with had never programmed herself to feel happy. She said didn't even know what happy was. So there was no way she could create a happy life for herself because she could not broadcast the frequency of feeling happy. She could feel sad and she could feel numb, but happy was something she never felt. That was pivotal for my research. With **PEP**, she could begin to program her mind to the emotion of happiness by bringing in pictures and things that stimulated her senses and felt good. She could go on to tell herself, "This feels good". Happy feels good. In a few weeks, she would shift her broadcast to feeling happy and then begin to manifest it in her life. The only way to create a new program in the mind is to bring it into the subconscious mind by repetition, stimulating the senses, and attaching an emotion to it using the conscious mind.

We are in one of three places with every emotion in the subconscious mind. We are programmed for a negative response or reaction, we are not programmed for it or **lack** it, or we broadcast the positive emotion.

Kids today are programmed to believe they are not safe unless they wear a bicycle helmet. One hundred years ago, people did not have that program. It didn't exist. People rode bikes and didn't consider needing a helmet. If we tell our kids to believe that they must wear a helmet or they are not safe, we could be adding mass or a link to the chain of *fear for safety*, depending on how they interpret that program and add emotion to it subconsciously.

Some kids become anxious without their helmet. They wouldn't consider being without their helmet for fear of safety. They attached the emotion of fear to the program. Then, some kids rebel. They wore the helmet when they were young because they had to, but as they got older, they ditched the helmet and believed they never needed it to begin with. They rejected the program and now have a negative attachment to it. Others believe that a helmet is probably a good idea. If they have one, that's fine, but if they don't have one, that's okay too. It doesn't define them. They don't have an opinion about it. The program isn't stuck in them. They lack emotional attachment to the program.

I believe our society collectively broadcasts the program of *fear for safety*. Bicycle helmets could be just one link in the chain. Think about your fears. What are they? What resonates with you? How long is your chain of *fear for safety*? How much mass does your fear for safety have? What are the things in your life that keep you stuck feeling fear?

Emotions are linked to programs. We want to keep positive programs. We want to release negative programs. When we can clearly discern the emotions that we have attached to these programs, we can chose to keep them or get rid of them. All of our programs are our truths. They are embedded in our minds. The linked emotions are stored in our hearts. The memories we have about them are stored in our brains. I have learned that we can reprogram ourselves to create different truths.

I was amazed and excited when I discovered we could actually lack a program.

For example:

I am sad. (Negative)
I don't know what it is like to be happy, or I'm not sad, but I'm not happy. (Lack)
I am happy. (Positive)

Negative –	Lack 0	Positive +
I need.	I don't care.	I am independent.
I am fearful.	I don't know.	I am safe.
I am not worthy.	I am numb.	I am worthy.
I fear criticism.	I am stuck.	I am confident.
I am not loved.	I don't feel it.	I am loved.

Are we programming our children for a positive life?

How do we spend our time? Does it make us feel positive or negative?

Do we envy others because they have an emotion we seem to lack?

Are you numb?

CHAPTER 16

~∾✦∾~

I Just Don't Get It!

Do you know someone who acts in a way that shocks you? Do they repeat the same behavior when you have brought it to their attention? Do you know someone who seems rude or careless? Do you say, "I don't understand how he could be that way" or "He is clueless"? Do you tell someone something a thousand times but always get the same response? Well here is the way **PEP** discerns that:

He is not programmed with an emotional response or reaction. He doesn't resonate with it either way. He doesn't feel it. He doesn't know how to act. **He doesn't get it.** That frequency is not broadcasted from his mind. It wasn't created. It doesn't exist, so he can't react or respond to it.

Until the person makes the conscious realization that he is missing a program and decides to create an emotional programmed response in his or her mind and store it in his heart, it isn't there.

We perceive people based on our senses. We may perceive that a person acts polite (positive), rude (negative), or doesn't know how to act (lacks the program).

I believe that parents and teachers who understand programming have the knowledge and power to program kids with positive frequencies when they are young. They also have the power to negatively program them.

Children who end up with legal or illegal addictions, depression, or in therapy are those who broadcast negative frequencies or lack the proper emotional response. Their subconscious is running their lives based on the programs they picked up in their environment as child. When they become consciously aware that they are on a negative program, they have the choice to change it to a different program. PEP is a great tool to shift negative programs to positive programs and to create missing programs.

When children are programmed with negative emotional frequencies, they create negative circumstances, events, and situations throughout their lives. They broadcast negative emotions, and the Law of Attraction magnetically returns matching frequencies.

If a child lacks an emotional response, his/her energy is influenced by the energy in their environment. Often, surrounding frequencies are negative. PEP uses spaced repetition and assimilation through the senses to create missing emotional programs.

When a child resonates with a negative emotional program like "I am not worthy", he unconsciously defines his life by that frequency. He creates his life and adds mass to that frequency. He experiences life link by link in a chain of events that match that emotion. Until his conscious mind realizes he is broadcasting, "I am not worthy", he vibrates in sympathetic resonance or harmony with that frequency, and he can't change it. His subconscious mind, by the *Law of Attraction*, brings circumstances and events that match the emotional frequency of *"I am not worthy"*, even if he consciously doesn't want them because he doesn't realize that he is broadcasting that with his emoter. To realize this is to bring it to reality or to the attention of the conscious mind.

We vibrate on a range of high to low frequencies depending on the emotional programs we broadcast. Drugs and low oxygen flow cause blocked energy and influence frequencies. Medications treat symptoms by influencing frequencies. Drugs don't release negative emotional programs or disperse the mass that created them. Drugs change the path of the energy. Poor-quality food and medication cause resistance that reroutes energy away from its natural flow. These things can lower a person's ability to broadcast and receive frequencies. Conversely, good nutrition, oxygenation and movement or exercise helps the free flow of energy and raises a person's ability to broadcast clear frequencies.

The wonderful thing about **Positive Emotional Programming** is that it identifies the negative and missing emotional program. It is a way to release negative programs, add missing positive programs, change the broadcast, and ultimately raise **vibration.** Vibration is defined as a person's emotional state. When our vibration rises, we broadcast positive emotional frequencies. When we broadcast positive emotional frequencies, our health and well-being improves. When our health and well-being improves, we broadcast positive emotions and create circumstances in our lives to magnetically attract more positive events.

CHAPTER **17**

◦◦◦◦◦◦

Energy of Emotion and
The Bible Analogy

I am convinced every one of us is a spiritual being, whether we consciously know it or not. In my journey to learn about the power of words and *everything is energy*, the Gospel of John in the Bible inspired me: *"In the beginning there was the Word."* I set out to read several versions of the Bible. I wanted to know the significance of "the Word". After reading Revelations and Genesis, I realized that there were uncanny similarities between what I read and what I was learning about energy.

What if *"the Word"* is the tool for expressing thought or emotion? So consider that *"In the beginning there was the Word"* could mean that, in the beginning, there was thought or emotion and thus the beginning of creation. If thoughts are energy made of particles, then words are the expression of those particles.

The words in the Bible differed from what I was learning about quantum physics, but the intention and the translations seemed the same. Here are a few of my favorite examples of the laws of the universe in congruence with the Bible:

"Ask and the door will be open, Seek and ye shall find."
—*Matthew 7:7-8*

The energetic translation: Questions open a circuit to the universe. Broadcast clear, concise, focused intention without resistance and you will get the answer in the form of a matching magnetic frequency.

"*What you sow, so shall ye reap.*"

—*Galatians 6:7*

The energetic translation: The emotion you broadcast is matching similar frequencies to give you circumstances that give you more of that emotion, or what you do comes back to you.

"*Forgive us our debts as we forgive our debtors.*"

—*The Lord's Prayer, Matthew 6:12*

The energetic translation: To forgive is to let go, to give up, or release. You must release stuck emotional programs to move forward and change your frequency. When we forgive, we create and attract forgiveness, release negative attachments and open the flow of energy.

"*Faith is the substance of things hoped for. The evidence of things not seen.*"

—*Hebrews 11:1*

The energetic translation: Substance is physical matter or mass. Evidence is to manifest or to make clear—manifesting matter from nonphysical to physical. It's adding mass to thought with emotion.

"*Judge not, that ye be judged.*"

—*Matthew 7:1*

The energetic translation: Broadcasting critical and negative emotions brings more of them right back to you by God/source and the Law of Attraction.

Why do courts have people swear to tell the truth? I believe that it is all about intentional emotional broadcasts. If one lies, the intention is deceit. Their broadcast is matched by like frequencies and brought back by the Law of Attraction. If this is true, then giving your word and keeping your word are powerful intentions, not to be taken lightly, and what you do really does come back to you!

CHAPTER 18

〜⸙〜

More Analogies

Here are some other analogies to create a clearer picture in your mind: *Direct a flashlight and a laser pen at a mirror:* Which light is more intense and stronger? The laser represents focused emotional frequency. A flashlight is not intense light. It spreads out. It represents a weaker frequency or confusion. You do the same thing when you think positively or negatively. Your intentions and emotions are either focused and intense, or scattered. *The more coherent and focused the frequency, either positive or negative, the faster and clearer it is picked up by like frequencies and brought back to you.*

Listen to the radio: You tune to station 102.1. You like what you hear. You do not have resistance to it. You harmonize with it. However, if you listen to 102.1 and you don't like what you hear, you are annoyed—not in resonance—and want to change the station. Your body may cringe, your brows may furrow, and your eyes may roll. You immediately select another station in the hope of finding something more appealing that you can agree to listen to and resonate with. *You broadcast the emotions that resonate with you.*

When you intend to watch channel 8, and your television is on channel 7, which is not a set station, you hear interference or static. The frequency is not clear, and you can't see what is playing. You are soon annoyed, and you quickly tune it to channel 8, so you can have a clear coherent frequency. You actually feel yourself calm down when the static or interference is cleared.

Clear, concise focus with emotion on what you want is the only way to get a clear concise match from the universe.

Your emoter is like your computer: It has different files on it. Each file is labeled with an emotion. You may have one labeled "Fear" and another labeled "Self-Esteem". Others are "Anger", "Guilt", or "Trust". In each of the files, you have stored a lifetime of experiences related to each emotion. Those are the documents. Open your file labeled "Fear." Every time in your life that you experience fear, you add another document to that file. Each document in the file has a title. One is *Fear of Flying;* others are *Fear of Criticism, Fear of Money, Fear of Lack, Fear of Dying,* and so on. Fear is an intense emotion. Traumas often accompany fear and can intensify the negative emotion. If you open a document, you can find the whole story of each fear and how the linked trauma happened. You also have files with no documents at all; you have not experienced it or assimilated an emotion. Your mind has memory. You have attached emotions to those memories.

The frequencies you broadcast are from the programs that you run. Negative emotional frequencies cause resistance and blockages that can ultimately lead to disease and dysfunction. Positive emotions allow the free flow of energy. When you feel stuck, you may not have a positive or a negative emotion attached; you are in confusion, static or you lack emotion. *Negative emotions stored in your memory are causing glitches in your mind, and that is what you broadcast and receive.*

CHAPTER 19

Programs Are Generational Like Chain Links

We take on energy from our ancestors and from our environment. Energy does not need to be seen or heard to influence our emotional frequency. We take on the energy of our ancestors emotionally through the subconscious programs that are passed on generationally. We can have programs stuck in us from generations back because we resonate and vibrate with the frequency of these programs from before birth without consciously knowing it. Along with our genetic code and physical body, we inherit energetic programs. We exist in the same energetic environment as our parents and ancestors. Therefore, by default, we resonate with positive and negative energetic frequencies from our relatives. Like it or not, want it or not, they are the gifts our parents and ancestors give us, and we don't consciously know it. It is subconscious.

Negative emotional programs often get stuck in our subconscious mind. Every time we experience a situation that makes us feel the same negative emotion again, we add another link to the chain. We forge a chain, link by link, with the emotions we broadcast and our response to them. We can feel the negative emotions in our body. Disease and dysfunction can begin to manifest where those emotions are stored as the chain gets longer and heavier. Often, we stick our emotions in the same place that our ancestors did, so disease appears genetic.

Do we get headaches because our fathers did? What if they weren't genetic? What if they were emotional blockages in the flow of energy? What if we took on the same negative programs and learned to put those negative emotions in our heads so that we could manifest headaches the same way dad did?

Once we realize that we take on our ancestors' energetic programs, they can be released and stopped from being passed on. We resonate with the environment we are in, and we co-create that environment with others. We live in the same environment with our family for the first several years of our life.

Are we co-creating our emotions and resonating with frequencies in a healthy environment?

What if addictions, diseases, and dysfunctions were programs or frequencies that get trapped or resonate with our emotional energy? What if they could be changed?

What if cancer was not a physical, genetic disease, but rather an energetic program? If everything is energy vibrating at different frequencies, then cancer must have a frequency and a likely attached emotional program. Could it be that simple? Could it be that there is not a single cure for cancer because we each have our own emotional programs?

If disease has an emotion or frequency attached to it, would the disease or dysfunction exist if the frequency were changed just like changing the channel of your television?

Could a technique like PEP that helps people find and release trapped emotional programs be the way to a solution?

"You are just like your mother."

—*Unknown*

"When you get to be my age, you will get this too!"

—*Unknown*

"You can tell what people are like by the company they keep."

—*Unknown*

"If you hang around them long enough, you will turn out just like them."
—*Unknown*

"I wear the chain I forged in life . . . I made it link by link, and yard by yard; I girded it in of my own free will, and of my own free will I wore it."
—*Jacob Marley in* A Christmas Carol *by Charles Dickens*

CHAPTER 20

❦

Step 1: Finding the Negative Emotion or Target

Finding the frequency of the emotion stuck in our mind is just like finding the right key on the piano. When we press a piano key, the string vibrates and makes the selected sound. We need to know which key to press.

To find the negative emotional frequency in the subconscious mind, we must think about the disease we are manifesting or focus on the situation that is causing the negative emotion. As we focus, just like the laser, we begin to clearly resonate on that frequency. It is what I call "finding the **target**". The chart on pages 76-77 is a guide to use with intuition to target broadcasted frequencies. **Intuition** is the ability to immediately understand something without the need for conscious reasoning. It is using emotion rather than rational thought to target the negative frequency.

When we don't feel a negative emotion at all, we may not be able to immediately access it. Focusing on a situation, another person, or a condition is how we gain access to the emotion attached to it. We often get a sense of heavy, low energy when we focus on a current condition, but many times we just can't find the words to describe the emotion we are feeling. That is because we are communicating with the subconscious mind. It works with feelings, not words. When we can find the words to express the emotion, we have taken the first step toward releasing the attached negative emotion by bringing it to the conscious mind and assigning a word to the emotion.

The list on pages 76-77 is designed to help find the emotion that is broadcasted and linked to the condition. With laser-focused thought, skim through the list. Your mind will resonate with one or more of the emotions. You are matching a frequency and creating a circuit to it.

Try This: Focus on a significant person in your life. Then skim through the list on pages 76-77. You feel nothing if you lack an attached emotion or a confirming "Aha" when you target a negative frequency.

When you think of that person, what do you feel? "I am not safe?" or "I feel frustrated?" or "I can't trust?"

Most people have a long chain of old emotional programs that influence relationships. Releasing these emotional programs will not only change how we perceive our relationships, but the other person will sense us differently. When we release a negative emotional frequency, we will no longer broadcast it, so the other person will no longer respond or react to it.

Using **PEP**, we break the circuit to the target emotional frequency and create a different circuit. When that happens, our relationships could feel different. We may disagree or we may not resonate with them until we adapt to the new frequency. Like changing a radio station, there could be static as we move from one frequency to another, or we may get along much better because the resistance is gone.

When we are not in good health, not experiencing success, or other unfulfilled desires, we broadcast negative or wrong frequencies. Some sort of resistance is present or we lack the program in the subconscious, emotional mind. We were designed to flow positive, high vibrational energy without resistance. Negative emotion is going against the flow and not aligned with who we are.

Take a look at the process I use for releasing a negative emotional program of extreme body pain such as fibromyalgia:

Focus on the pain. Create a mind movie and actually feel the pain throughout your body. Then, using your intuition or muscle testing, and pages 76-77 of this book, locate the target frequency that is being broadcasted. Write down the negative target frequency and then all of the feelings and situations that come up in your mind linked to this pain.

I worked with a woman who was broadcasting *fear of safety*. I was able to trace her fear to age 5. She discerned that she was abused at age 5.

Once the emotions attached to abuse like *fear for safety* were brought to the conscious mind, she could analyze and release the negative emotional attachment to them. I coached her to release the negative attached emotion using the process on pages 76-77 of this book. The words and phrases on pages 78-79 are loaded with mass, creating power. We used the mass that we created to move the emotion from her subconscious mind, releasing the magnetic attachment. She deleted the document from the file using powerful words along with acupressure. She said her pain went away.

I have had success coaching people to release emotional resistances linked to symptoms of severe body pain like fibromyalgia, sciatica, migraine, chronic pain anywhere, fears, fear of flying, eating disorders, fear of criticism, depression, abuse, allergies, food allergies, panic, sadness, grief, memory loss, anxiety, loss of job, lack of money, fear of failure, postsurgical pain and discomfort, PMS, knee pain, hip pain, hot flashes, insomnia, grief, addiction, arthritis, digestive disorders, relationship upsets, and symptoms like those of diabetes and many other programs.

PEP finds the negative emotional target. It translates emotions into words and gives them mass with focused thought. Then, PEP brings the attached emotions from subconscious to the conscious mind. The conscious mind rationalizes the emotion and finds words to describe it. Finally, PEP releases the magnetic attachment and pushes the negative emotion out of the magnetic field. Sometimes, people immediately forget what emotion they were releasing. When that happens, I know it was released.

If a science teacher can have amazing results with **Positive Emotional Programming**, *imagine what a scientist with good intentions and technology could do for releasing emotional resistance linked to disease and dysfunction like anxiety, addiction, abuse, learning issues, blockages to success, and much more.*

"You cannot solve a problem with the same mind that created it."
—Einstein

Can you use your "other mind" to solve your own challenges?

Could obesity be misdirected energy? Resistance? Or a missing emotional program? What about . . .

Addiction?	Abuse?	Lack of love?	Stress?	Poverty?	Money?
ADD?	Crime?	Fears?	Illness?	Loneliness?	Hot flashes?
Autism?	Depression?	Anxiety?	Abuse?	Allergies?	Chronic pain?

CHAPTER **21**

Circuits and EFT

I believe that, once the emotional resistance is identified, it can be released and the frequency can be changed. An analogy to circuits may help us understand this concept further.

To create a **circuit**, we must have a power source and conduit to send the charge of electricity and turn on a light. The conduit must be free of resistance to allow the current to flow. If it encounters resistance, the energy is rerouted or stopped.

Positive Emotional Programming is like finding the resistance in a circuit, releasing it, and then creating the correct circuit. When electrical wires are covered or frayed, they reroute, stop, or have static interference. In the body, the energy is misdirected or trapped. The body reacts or responds to the new path. Using powerful words and focused intention, **Positive Emotional Programming** moves trapped energy, opens pathways, and reprograms emotional frequencies, creating a clear path for energy to flow. Ideally, the emotional frequencies are reprogrammed to what they were intended to be from the beginning.

EMOTIONAL FREEDOM TECHNIQUE

EFT is a remarkable technique that uses acupressure by tapping your fingers on energy meridians to release resistance from the body. At this point, you may wish to go online and look into EFT or *Emotional Freedom Technique.* You only need a basic understanding to continue.

I recommend *The Tapping Solution* by Jessica, Alex, and Nick Ortner. Many other tapping teachers have YouTube videos about EFT. Check out The Tapping Solution. A link to it can be found at my website: ***www. amopublishing.com/bookstore/Energy-of-Emotion.***

Miraculous things are happening as a result of Dr. Roger Callahan's Thought Field Therapy and Gary Craig's EFT tapping techniques. Tapping is a way of communicating with the subconscious mind. Tapping helps move energy and communicates with the subconscious mind to release negative emotional programs and reset them to the desired positive frequencies. It works well in conjunction with **PEP**.

Please research and understand EFT acupressure.

The acupressure points that I prefer are as follows:

KC = Karate chop point or the side of hand

TE = Third eye or eyebrow

SE = Side of eye

UE = Under the eye

UN = Under the nose

C = Chin

CB = Collar Bone

UA = Under the arm

TH = Top of the head

W = Grab wrist

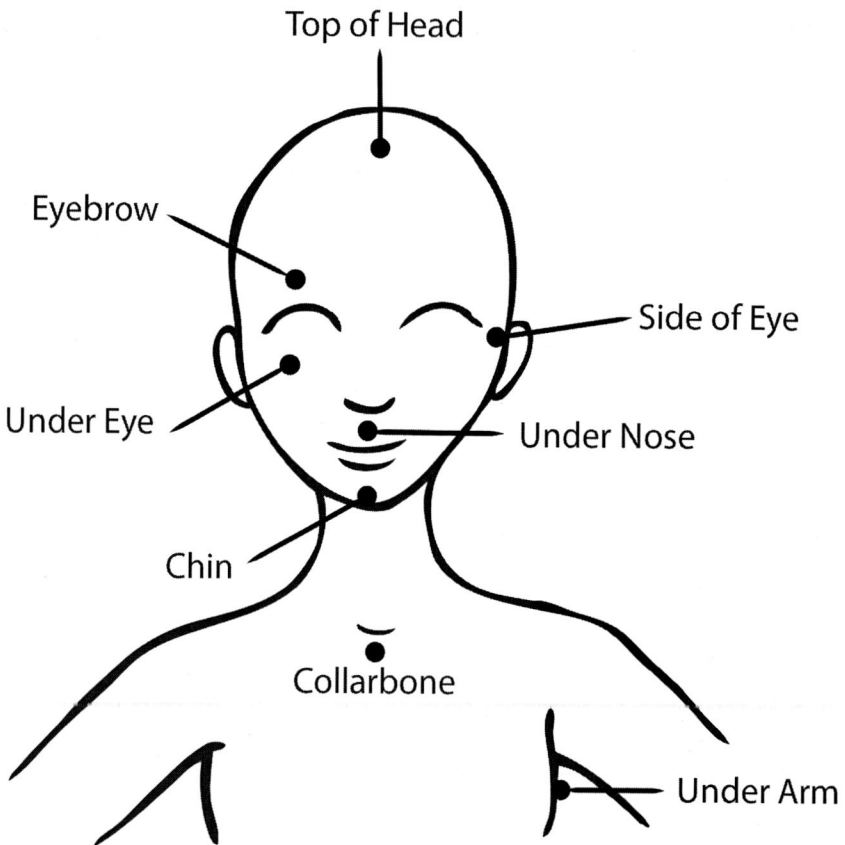

Top of Head

Eyebrow

Side of Eye

Under Eye

Under Nose

Chin

Collarbone

Under Arm

CHAPTER 22

❦

The Path to Freedom

You can target negative emotional programs with any one of these three methods. I suggest that you start with using your intuition and then experiment with the other methods.

1. Use the chart on pages 76-77 in this book and your intuition to identify and target negative emotional programs.
2. Use the chart on pages 76-77 in this book and yes/no responses with muscle testing to identify and target negative emotional programs.
3. Try dowsing or divining (see page 92) for details to target negative emotional programs.

Once we identify the emotion, we have a target. Let's say we are broadcasting the fear "I don't feel safe". Ask yourself, "What is stopping me from feeling safe? What do I believe about this?" Think about that fear. Then begin to create a movie in the conscious mind about all of the times in your life that you didn't feel safe. Every event is a link in the chain or a document in the file of that emotional program. When we begin to feel a strong emotion or discomfort in our body, that is a good sign that we found the target. We can feel the resistance in our body like a dam building up water pressure; we are giving it mass. The stronger we feel the emotion, the bigger the release. Giving it mass gives us a larger target to hit.

Now, using a pencil, write down all of the events in your life that come to your mind that made you feel that you were not safe. Writing things down gives them mass. It is important to write so your mind can focus on the events that caused this emotion. The goal is to focus on them intensely, enlarge the target, then push the mass out of your mind. Get the feeling to well up in your body. You need to focus your thoughts so you can release the emotions attached to them. Remember there is an equal and opposite reaction for every action. As your emotion gets stronger, you are bringing it to consciousness. The stronger you focus, the more clarity you will have. The goal is to match the frequency and then release it, just like the opera singer breaks the glass.

As you play the movie, you may feel pains, discomfort, or even irritation in your body. That is where you stored that emotion. It is also where diseases may go if you keep adding links.

Locate and rate the discomfort on a scale from 1 to 10. Intention should be clear, focused, and sustained for at least a 60-second period for the subconscious mind to find it, add mass, and set up for the release. It is like blowing up a balloon and then popping it.

Disclaimer: You take responsibility for anything that comes up in your mind if you decide to proceed through this process.

Effects include, but are not limited to:

Crying	Goose bumps	Confusion	Cognitions	Feeling very calm
Laughing	Lightness	Vivid dreams	Enlightenment	Tiredness
Anger	Sadness	Release	Relief	Energy boost
Frustration	Feeling empty	Hopefulness	Yawning	Different feeling

The next page will take you through the process of releasing a sample target emotion. Worksheets found on pages 76-79 of this book are provided for you to use on your target negative emotional programs. Use them over and over to release negative emotional programs.

CHAPTER **23**

჻ᏽ჻

Step 2: The Process for Releasing Negative Emotional Attachments

There are many styles of EFT. For this example, I have created a combination of powerful, intentional phrases that appeal to the emotions and words that create mass in the mind. It works best to say them aloud, because you are using the sense of hearing and sound vibrations along with the emotions. Do your best to feel them while stimulating acupressure points using EFT. I modify these words when I find more powerful words.

▓ READ THIS ENTIRE SECTION BEFORE TRYING THIS ON YOUR OWN.

First, find a place where you will be undisturbed for several minutes. After you have identified the negative emotional target, you must own it, accept it, and acknowledge it. You must fully bring it to your consciousness and give it mass to release it and let it go. This can get uncomfortable.

For our example: Begin to create a movie in your mind "Fear for my safety". Go all the way back through your life. Own it. Live it. Ask yourself, "What is stopping me from feeling safe? What are my beliefs about this?"

Using a pencil, write a laundry list of all of the times you can remember fearing for your safety. Take a moment to sense any pain or discomfort in your body. Rate that pain from 1 to 10.

For example:
"*I am not safe.*" I feel a tightness in my chest. It is an *8* on a scale of *1 to 10*.

■■ TAKE THREE SLOW, DEEP BREATHS TO GET THE
■■ OXYGEN FLOWING THROUGH YOUR BODY
AND GET THE ENERGY IN MOTION.

Then, tap the side of your hand and say out loud:
"Even though *I am not feeling safe,* I can accept how I feel."
"Even though I am broadcasting the frequency of *I am not safe,* I acknowledge it and I take responsibility for it."
"Even though I am transmitting the frequency of *I am not safe,* I can see that now.

■■ CONTINUE TO PLAY YOUR MIND MOVIE AND LOOK AT WHAT
■■ YOU WROTE DOWN. SAY THE FOLLOWING PHRASES OUT
LOUD, EMPHASIZING THE BOLD WORDS:

Eyebrow: "***I don't feel safe.*** Release resistance and let it go."
Side of Eye: "***I really don't feel safe,*** for these reasons right here. (Look at the list.) Release resistance and let it go."
Under Eye: "***I am not safe;*** that is my truth. Release resistance and let it go."
Under Nose: "***I am not safe;*** that is my reality. Release resistance and let it go."
Chin: "I am afraid ***I am not safe.*** Release resistance and let it go."
Collar Bone: "***My body is not safe.*** Release resistance and let go of the fear."
Under arm: "***I don't feel safe.*** Release resistance and let it go."
Top of head: "***I am not safe.*** Release resistance and let it go."

■■ NEXT, TAKE YOUR TIME TO THINK ABOUT AND THEN FEEL THESE
■■ WORDS AS YOU SPEAK THEM ALOUD. FOCUS ADDS MASS.
TAP ONLY THE THIRD EYE. (BETWEEN YOUR EYES):

• What do I need to do to release this belief?

• Why am I stuck on this frequency?

- What is stopping me from releasing the belief that I am not safe?
- Everything that I have done to create this belief—whether it seemed right, wrong, good, bad, reward, or punishment when I created it—I will destroy and un-create it on all layers, all links, and all levels.
- Cancel and un-create all misunderstood agreements with regard to fear for my safety, past, present, future, and all throughout my timeline.
- Cut energetic connection in, on, and around my body to this fear.
- Match the frequency, tone, and vibration to this fear. Shatter the resistance.
- Open the energy flow through time, space, and reality.
- Break the chain to this and any inherited programs, beliefs, or imprints at the point of creation, point of limitation, and point of destruction of self.
- Find the target and shatter the mass of negative emotion that I attached to it.
- Transmute emotions linked to this fear back to energy.
- Allow the free flow of energy through my mind and body.
- Remove all resistance.
- Wash away negative attachments.
- Open and clear the pathways of fear for my safety from all systems.
- Take out and take away pathogens.
- Balance my mind, body, and spirit.
- I ask my body to let go of this and all linked emotions.
- I ask God/source to make this fear never return.
- I ask for forgiveness and I offer forgiveness for accepting this and staying stuck in it throughout my timeline.
- I choose to allow this to flow right through and out of me.

(*You can modify these statements. The words I have discovered have strong resonance, focus, and add mass. This is just a guide. I am sure there are other word. In fact, I edit this list quite often.*)

TAKE A DEEP BREATH, GRAB YOUR WRIST, AND LET IT
OUT. PAUSE, REST, AND EVALUATE HOW YOU FEEL NOW.
I RECOMMEND DRINKING PLENTY OF WATER DURING THIS
PROCESS TO KEEP THE FLOW OF ENERGY AND OXYGEN
GOING THROUGH YOU.

Remember this: When we find ourselves in highly emotional situations, we
are vibrating the attached emotion with strong, laser-like focus. It is a big
negative target. It is an excellent opportunity to release the negative emotion and then reprogram our mind to a positive thought. Focusing with
strong emotion on what we want begins to give it mass. Strong negative or
positive emotion creates a highly focused broadcast. Releasing when we are
highly emotional will give us an equal and opposite release. We need to use
those moments to our advantage. We can get enormous movement of energy
and relief when we identify, focus intention and emotion, then release and
change embedded frequencies this way.

> "*Feel your anger; it makes you focus, makes you stronger.*"
> —*Emperor Palpatine to Darth Vader, Star Wars, Episode VI*

CHAPTER 24

❧

Feeling a Shift and PEP

Assess how you feel. Often, you will feel a sense of calm. Some people react with laughter, yawns, tears, goose bumps, or even annoyance. Some people sense a feeling of quiet, like the static has cleared. At this point, there is a shift, a release, or movement of energy. Assess your target emotion. How does it feel now when you say, *"I fear for my safety"*? Does it feel farther away? Or not true anymore? Is it still there? Where does it rank now on the scale of 1 to 10?

Take a look at the list you wrote and read each line. You will know if you still feel a charge. If you are annoyed, you are broadcasting a negative emotion. It is an indication that there is more to release. If it just feels like a bunch of words, you've released the emotional attachment.

Cross off those things that don't feel real anymore. If it still feels real, you may wish to repeat the process. If you still feel something well up in you, it's possible that you brought up a different emotion, and you may need to scan the list on pages 76-77 to find it. Repeat the process if you find another negative emotional target.

When you finish, tear up the list that you wrote in pencil and say out loud, "This is past. It is over." Do your best to really feel that and believe it.

■■
■■ *IT IS EXTREMELY IMPORTANT TO "CHANGE YOUR MIND" TO A POSITIVE THOUGHT AND THEN REPROGRAM YOUR EMOTIONS WITH SPACED REPETITION AND AFFIRMATIONS WITH PEP.*

After releasing the negative emotion from our mind, it is likely that we are in that place of lack where we don't feel the positive or the negative emotional program. **It is imperative to focus on Positive Emotional Programs.** When we have a release, we actually leave a gaping hole in the magnetic field of our mind where that negative emotion was. We sometimes feel numb or nothing after we release the attached emotion. Remember, emotions are magnetic, and the next emotion we feel will fill the hole and we will begin to create from that emotion. The goal is to be sure that our brain is focused on positive thoughts and our heart broadcasts positive emotions. Otherwise, we create more negative thoughts, add negative emotions, and then create more by the magnetic law of attraction.

> *Consider what happens when we pray or dwell on a negative circumstance with focused thought. We begin to create more of it and attach emotions to it. We give it mass. We resonate with it. We begin to own that emotion at the quantum level.*
>
> *Are parents and schools educating kids to resonate with positive frequencies? What emotional programs do kids have regarding school? Are the books they read raising their vibration? Or do they bring them down? What is intended by teaching sad or scary information?*
>
> *If kids are sitting in front of a screen all day, what is the programming? Everything that the parents and schools do with children adds links to their emotional chains and mass to their emotional programs, and most people don't even consciously know it.*
>
> *When we are given a diagnosis, do we agree to take it? Do we begin to resonate with it and then create it by focusing on it? What if we rejected it and forgot about it?*

❦

CHAPTER 25

What Now?

Y ou are no longer broadcasting the frequency "*I am not safe*". It is likely you are in that area between the positive and negative emotion. You no longer feel "not safe", but you don't feel safe either. It would be appropriate to replace that emotional frequency and broadcast the belief "*I am safe*".

As infants, when first created, we were intended to be vibrating pure, high, positive frequencies. Then, as we experienced life, we picked up the frequencies around us and attached emotion to them. Many of our embedded frequencies started before the age of 7. We can locate the **Positive Emotional Program** that was suppressed under the negative program we just released. It is like asking our mind to remember back to a time when we broadcasted a different frequency. What is missing? Often, it is just the opposite feeling. In this case, it would be **"Faith that I am safe"**. Is that missing from your mind?

To find the desired positive emotion, use your intuition or muscle testing, and turn to pages 81-82 of this book to go through the list of positive emotions. You will get the "Aha" feeling with intuition, or you may just feel most comfortable reprogramming yourself with the opposite emotion, "I believe I am safe or I have faith that I am safe".

*What if teachers could educate students to release negative programming with **PEP**?*

*What if schools implemented a program like **Positive Emotional Programming** to release old programs and replace them with desirable, healthy, success programs?*

What if behavioral issues were just negative embedded programs that could be released?

Why does a criminal get out of jail and repeat the same crime? Why does a child repeat the same unwanted behavior? He is programmed on that emotional frequency. He cannot "not" do it until he brings it to consciousness, analyzes it, releases it, and changes the frequency.

Why can't an addict quit, even when she can rationalize that the habit is wrong? She is subconsciously programmed on that frequency and cannot "not" do it until she realizes the attached subconscious emotional program and releases it. She can't release it if she doesn't know that she has it.

Why do people gain weight back after losing it? They have not changed their frequency. They cannot "not" gain it back until they find and release the linked emotional program.

Why is it common for abused children to have parents who were abused? They are all on that frequency. They harmonize with it. They cannot "not" abuse until they identify the program, release attached emotions, and broadcast a different emotion. When they do that, they stop it from being passed on.

CHAPTER 26

You Were Born That Way

It makes sense to me that we were supposed to be born free and clear of negative frequencies. But as life happens, we suppress the positive frequencies with negative thoughts and beliefs, or we never get a positive program at all. Infant—infinite. As we grow up, negative programming suppresses the emotions that God/source intended.

A child sees the world as absolute truth, and everything that happens is interpreted by the subconscious mind as normal and acceptable, because the subconscious cannot rationalize and does not judge. Its only job is to feel with emotion and then broadcast frequencies. When a child born with the frequency "I am safe" is abused, the subconscious mind creates resistance and redirects to the frequency of abuse due to the trauma associated with the abuse. The subconscious mind broadcasts frequencies of abuse, and then like frequencies are magnetically attracted back to the child. It almost appears that the child wants abuse, because abuse is the frequency being broadcasted and matched by the subconscious mind.

As the child grows up, he continues to attract circumstances, events, and situations to make him feel abused. He adds mass and a link to that chain each time he experiences more abuse. Before long, he has a long chain of abusive experiences. He can live his whole life attracting all sorts of physical, mental, emotional, or sexual abuse. The subconscious mind does not discern right, wrong, good, or bad. It matches frequencies based on emotions and by the magnetic law of attraction; circumstances that match that frequency are returned.

When a person's subconscious mind is **re-minded** with **PEP** of the intended frequency of *"I am safe"*, it can recreate that emotional frequency and start to attract circumstances, events, and situations that make him feel safe. However, **I have learned that, when reprogramming to a positive frequency, it takes time to get the subconscious mind to resonate with the positive emotional program. It does not become a part of us without conscious effort and spaced repetition. Just like a new idea, it needs to be developed before it becomes something. A changed frequency is weak at first. We must often focus with intense emotion to assimilate at the quantum level. Focus gives it mass. Dr. Emoto's experiment suggested that the frequencies put in water can be changed or even disappear if not focused upon. A frequency must be consciously broadcasted until it resonates subconsciously.**

It takes at least two weeks of Positive Emotional Programming to create a habit. A habit happens when a repeated action harmonizes at the quantum energetic level. By reprogramming the positive emotion with repetition through the senses, the conscious mind will begin to reprogram the subconscious mind. Creating a movie, using imagination, immersion, and bringing the feelings into the mind through the senses with intense emotion is ideal because the subconscious mind cannot tell the difference between imagination and reality.

Could it be that we cannot create wealth in our lives until our cells are vibrating on the frequency of wealth?

If we have never known wealth, could we manifest it by releasing the emotions attached to poverty then creating a habit through repetition and immersing ourselves in a wealthy environment?

Do wealthy people stay wealthy because they stay in an environment of wealth and therefore vibrate on that frequency effortlessly? Is wealth in their cells?

Could that be why people also stay in poverty?

Are people who are broke vibrating poverty at the molecular level?

Do they pass it on generationally in their cells?

CHAPTER 27

◈

Step 3: Reprogramming with PEP, Positive Emotional Programming

Now, using white paper and a blue pen, write "I have faith that I am safe" or the **Positive Emotional Program** from pages 81-82 that you wish to create. Then, continue to write how it would feel if it were true. For example:

> I have faith that I am safe.
>
> I can feel calm.
>
> I have all I need to be safe.
>
> I can relax.
>
> It is over.
>
> I can move on in my life.
>
> If I am safe, I can focus on other things.
>
> I am protected.
>
> All is well.

Write in positive terms. Stay away from inversions like "I **don't** have to worry any more". Your subconscious mind will only focus on the worry. It doesn't process words like "don't". Think about the words you are using and their meaning. Keep it simple and direct.

CHAPTER 28

❧

Positive Emotional Programming (PEP)

To reset to the positive emotional program, tap your third eye (between your eyes) with one hand and say these words backed by strong emotion. Emphasize the bold words (the stronger you can feel them, the more mass you give them and the stronger the transmission of frequency):

- I am **thankful and grateful** to focus my thoughts on feeling safe now.
- **The past is over.** I am safe now.
- What if I could really **feel** safe?
- What would it **look** like?
- What would it **sound** like?
- What would it **smell** like?
- What would it **taste** like?
- What if I could plant the seeds of safety and allow the seeds to grow?
- What if I could **believe** that I am safe now?
- What if I could **remember** what it is like to feel safe?
- What if I could have **faith** that I am safe?

- What if I could **allow** myself to feel safe?
- What if all I had to do was **ask** to feel safe?
- It is **possible** to feel safe.
- I **think** I can feel safe.
- I **choose** to feel safe.
- I would **love** to feel safe.
- I **choose to broadcast** a frequency of feeling safe.
- Show me the next logical step toward feeling safe. Make it easy, obvious, and fast.
- I **allow** myself to receive circumstances and people that make me feel safe.
- I **co-create** this feeling with God/source.
- **I invite** this feeling into me from my head to my chest to my abdomen, legs, feet, and ground to the earth and back through me in a circuit.
- I am **transmitting and receiving** the feeling of safety.
- I am in **harmony** with feeling safe.
- I **agree** to feel safe.
- I **feel** safe now. This is my truth.
- I **radiate** safety.
- I am worthy of feeling safe.
- The past is over. I **focus** on feeling safe now.
- I am **now** programmed to feel safe.
- And so be it. Let it be done. Make it so it will be done from this day forward. **Thank you.**

The intention behind the **PEP** statements is to reprogram the conscious mind with thoughts in the brain using the senses and influence the emotions broadcasted from the heart. It is the goal to get the mind and body resonating and vibrating on the frequencies of the positive emotion. "What if" questions open a circuit and allow the conscious mind to rationalize and complete the circuit with a positive thought. Notice that I use the word "feel" over and over. Feelings are appealing to the subconscious mind and the heart.

Statements in present time tell the mind to apply this new broadcast right now. Expressing thankfulness brings positive thoughts to the brain. Expressing gratitude brings positive emotions to the heart. Gratitude is a powerful subconscious emotion.

Just as programs are created by repetition, the new frequency must be thought about and dwelled upon for it to create mass in the mind. In Dr. Emoto's experiment, he also found that the crystalline structure of the water can be changed with another thought or a different attached emotion. Until the habit of a positive thought is created, it is subject to change, or more likely it will not be formed because it doesn't have enough mass or attached emotion. Habits are embedded frequencies. They have attached emotions. When they are deeply embedded, they become a part of you at the quantum energetic level. **Therefore, it is imperative that you use lots of reminders of the new emotional frequency until it is embedded, effortless, automatic, and part of you. You cannot broadcast an emotion that you don't feel. Repeat the positive statements and visualize outcomes several times a day for a minimum of two weeks.**

Try these strategies for programming yourself and to broadcast positive emotion.

- Repeat the positive process on pages 83-84 twice a day for at least two weeks, morning and night.

- Read pages 83-84 in the alpha state, which is before bed and upon rising.

- Read the list you wrote in blue pen over and over.

- Use note cards or sticky notes with the statements posted everywhere.

- Bless a piece of jewelry or your watch with the new program so you are reminded of it every time you look at that item.

- Be aware of your thoughts. Catch yourself thinking negative thoughts, tell yourself "no" or "stop" or "cancel", and quickly shift them to your new program.

- Instead of worrying about the worst scenario, think about the best scenario.

- "*What if*" yourself into positive thoughts: "What if it is over, and I am safe?" "What if I do get that job?" "What if I am well?" "What if I was thin?"

- Immerse yourself in an environment where you can sense and feel the positive emotional frequency you are trying to create. You will begin to resonate with it. It becomes a habit and part of you at the energetic level because you are living, breathing, tasting, smelling, feeling, seeing, and sensing it with all of your senses and giving it mass and then attaching emotion.

The key is to feel good when you do this. If you feel doubt or fear, it cannot be created; you will get circumstances of doubt or fear.

"Surround yourself with positive people."

—Unknown

"The only thing we have to fear is fear itself."

—Franklin D. Roosevelt

"If you hang around them long enough, you will turn out just like them."

—Unknown

"You become what you think about most of the time."

—Earl Nightingale

What if we spent more time focusing on a positive outcome than a negative outcome?

Afterword

It has been my intention to give you a basic understanding of **PEP, Positive Emotional Programming**. With practice, you can educate yourself to do it accurately and help others. **Be sure that you ask permission before trying this on anyone. Often, people are not ready to let go of their negative emotional programs even when we can see they could benefit. There is some discomfort in letting go of what is familiar. Some people are not ready for PEP.** Please use the following pages as a guide to release your unwanted programs and reset to **Positive Emotional Programs.** Some people prefer to do this with a friend, because it seems easier for others to sense what we are broadcasting. Others are looking in from the outside.

We can find negative emotional programs using intuition when we are in tune to our emotions. Muscle testing is another method of locating the negative broadcasts. Talk therapy may help identify resistance as well.

We can infer the frequency that people broadcast by listening to what they are talking about. Just sense the emotion they attach to what they say. Are they constantly talking about their bad health? They are probably broadcasting *fear of ill health or fear of dying.*

I believe that a pendulum is the most accurate way for finding the trapped emotional programs in the subconscious mind, but using a pendulum takes training and practice. Many people don't understand how it works, so they dismiss it. The accuracy of translating subconscious frequencies into words with a pendulum is miraculous for me. It is amazing—what we don't know. See page 92 for more on this.

If everything is energy and emotions are created, moveable, quantifiable, changeable THINGS made of particles that have mass, what would happen if, collectively, humanity DID nothing but reprogram thoughts and gave mass to positive frequencies regarding education, religion, war, economics, govern-ment, family, and coworkers?

What are your truths and values? Are they positive, negative, or do you even have them?

Think about the emotions you feel. Those are frequencies you are broadcasting. That is what you will receive. Do you want it?

Be sure to understand the meaning of the words that you use. They are powerful. The words you use express the emotions you are broadcasting.

I urge you to consider the power of words, thoughts and intention . . . but mostly the energy of emotion.

I appreciate your time and thoughtful attention.

Your **PEP** Coach,
Donna

Negative Emotional Programs

Process for Intuition, Muscle Testing, or Pendulum Yes/No

Focus on a situation, disease, or dysfunction on your mind. Ask yourself these questions for a yes or no response. **Preface what you say with "I believe_____."**

I feel betrayed	I am overwhelmed	I am out of control
I feel ill	I lack the will to live	I am unhappy
I fear poverty	I feel responsible	I lack strength
I fear criticism	I feel accountable	I am unlovable
I fear ill health	I feel bored	I am being critical
I fear loss of love	I fear rejection	I lack faith
I fear old age	I feel lack	I feel rejected
I fear death	I feel rage	I am unworthy
I live in doubt	I am a failure	I can't get it right
I live in indecision	I have a poor body image	I feel stuck
I resist change	I am unable to focus	I am feeling revengeful
I fear for my safety	I am suicidal	I am in denial
I feel hatred	I fear failure	I am unsuccessful
I am angry	I fear loss	I don't belong
I feel shame	I fear people	I am undeserving
I feel guilty	I'm not going to get it	I am sabotaging myself
I am frustrated	I'm not good enough	I feel unmotivated
I lack trust	I am influenced by others	I lack inspiration
I feel controlled	I am unwanted	I lack willpower

I envy_____	I lack acknowledgment	I lack belief
I am codependent	I fear abandonment	I fear leaving
I feel helpless	I lack protection	I lack direction
I am irritated	I am a terrible parent	I am discouraged
I am depressed	I fear having _____	I am impatient
I feel anxious	I lack support	I am full of blame
I am obsessing	I lack purpose	I am worried
I am a victim	I am abused	I feel overwhelmed
I cannot forgive	I feel enslaved	I am restless
I am selfish	I lack freedom	I feel grieving
I am disappointed	I feel resentful	I feel pessimistic
I am disgusted	I fear being alone	I feel desperate
I am sad	I fear taking action	I am addicted
I feel panic	I need _____	I lack money
I am jealous	I feel pain	I feel fat
I feel deceit	I feel pressure	I am too thin
I am abused	I lack confidence	I am sick about _____
I am bitter	I lack love	Name the condition _____
I regret _____	I fear the future	I fear success

(Reproducible)

Negative Emotional Release Statements

(Make copies of this page to use over again
when different emotions emerge.)

**Fill the blanks with one target emotion selected
from the list on pages 76-77.**

Starting now, go back through your life, thinking about the times that you felt _____. The stronger you feel the emotion/belief, the bigger the release. Ask yourself: **"What are my beliefs about this? How do I feel about this?"** As you play the movie, you may feel pains, discomfort, tightness, or even irritation. Use a pencil to write down a laundry list of every event that made you feel that emotion. Make a mental note of where you feel discomfort, and rate it on a scale of 1 to 10. For example:

I feel/believe _____. I feel it in my _____. It is a _____ on a scale of 1 to 10.

Take three slow, deep breaths to get the oxygen flowing through you.

Starting with any current thoughts, create a movie back through childhood focusing on _____. Tap the side of your hand and say out loud:

"Even though **I feel/believe** _____, I can accept that."
"Even though I am **broadcasting the frequency** of _____, I acknowledge it and I take responsibility for it."

"Even though I believe/feel_____ I understand that now."

With the one hand, tap through these acupressure points while saying these phrases out loud: **Emphasize the bold words.** The stronger you can feel them as you say them, the stronger the transmission of frequency and the better the release.

Change the words to "I feel or I believe", wherever it feels right for you.

Eyebrow: "I **am** _____, release resistance, let it go."

Side of eye: "I **know I am** _____, release resistance, let it go."

Under eye: "I **am** _____; this is my truth, release resistance, let it go."

Under nose: "I **know I feel** _____; this is my reality; release resistance, let go."

Chin: "I **created** _____, release it and let it go.

Collar bone: "I **feel** _____ in my body, release resistance, let it go."

Under arm: "I **believe I am** _____, release resistance, let it go."

Top of head: "I **really feel** _____, release resistance, let it go."

(Reproducible)

Tap the third eye. Say these phrases out loud with focus and emotion:

- What do I need to do to release resistance to _____?
- What is stopping me from letting go of _____?
- Why am I stuck feeling _____?
- Right, wrong, good, bad, reward, or punishment, for all the reasons I created this, I will destroy and un-create it now.*
- Cancel all misunderstood words with regard to _____.
- Match the frequency, tone, and vibration to _____. Release the resistance.

- Cut the energetic cords and break the circuit to _____.
- Take out and take away attached pathogens.
- Find the target and shatter the mass of negative emotion I attached to it.
- Break the chain to this and any linked inherited programs beliefs or imprints at the:
  - Point of creation.
  - Point of limitation.
  - Point of destruction of self.
- I'm asking my mind and body to let go of this and all linked emotions.
- I'm asking God/source to take it away and may it never return.
- Transmute linked negative emotions and beliefs back to energy.
- Wash away negative emotional attachments.
- Open the energy flow through time, space, and reality.
- Open and clear energetic pathways in all body systems.
- Allow the free flow of energy through my mind and body.
- Balance my mind, body, and spirit.
- I ask for forgiveness and I offer forgiveness for staying stuck in this throughout my timeline.
- I forgive anyone and anything that helped me to create it.
- I choose to allow the free flow of energy right through and out of me.

**Take a deep breath, grab your wrist, and let out your breath.
Look at the list again and re-asses.**

This phrase is quoted and edited from Access Consciousness, www.accessconsciousness.com.

(Reproducible)

Positive Emotional Programs

(Select from affirmations such as these to replace the negative programs.)

Use the opposite emotion from the list of negative programs or select from this list to reprogram your mind. Choose one you can begin to believe. If you can't even begin to believe it, you can't create it. To make them feel more believable, preface them with:

I will consider that__. I ask myself to believe__. What if__. It is over, _____ now.

I am rich	I appreciate	I feel good
I chose abundance	I am willing to change	I am willing
I am prosperous	I am grateful	I feel secure
I am wealthy	I am thankful	I am in present time
I am confident	I feel joyful	I have faith
I am healthy	I create _____	I love myself
My body is optimum	I co-create	I can love others
I am healed	I believe	I can let go
I am in love	I choose to _____	I am secure
I am safe	I want _____	I am encouraged
It is over	I desire _____	I am willing _____
I am flexible	I am moving forward	I am content
I enjoy life	I can have _____	I have integrity
I feel young	I can be _____	I can allow _____
I look young	I can do _____	I can appreciate _____
I feel great	I am empowered	I can accept _____
I feel fantastic	I am successful	I know _____

Things are going my way	I have purpose	Life is everlasting
I feel love	I have direction	I am forgiven
I am happy	I am doing God's/ source's will	I can focus
I am hopeful	I am powerful	I am smart
I can trust	I am happy	I am capable
I am calm	I have courage	I am loved
I am peaceful	I feel serene	I can move forward
All is well	I feel harmony	I am persistent
I have integrity	I am enlightened	I think I can feel ____
I am in control	I feel accomplishment	I feel empowered
I am proactive	I am worthy	I am satisfied
I cause	I am patient	I feel peace
I am excited	I am perseverant	I think I can have___
I am free	I am enlightened	I think I can be___
I am confident	I am compassionate	I am fine

Add your own: _____

(Reproducible)

Positive Emotional Programming Statements

In blue pen, write the **Positive Emotional Program** that you wish to create. Keep that with you or hang it up where you can read it over and over. You must give it mass in your mind.

As you speak these affirmations, fill in the blanks with your **Positive Emotional Program** from pages 81-82. Create a new mind movie. Using one hand, tap your third eye and with strong emotion say:

- I am thankful and grateful to focus and begin to feel _____.
- What if I could really feel_____?
- What would it look like?
- What would it sound like?
- What would it smell like?
- What would it taste like?
- What if I could plant a seed of _____ and allow the seed to grow?
- What if I could believe that I am/have_____?
- What if I could believe that I am/have_____?
- What if I could remember what it is like to feel_____?
- What if it were safe to feel_____?
- What if I could have faith that I am/have_____?
- What if I could allow myself to have/be_____?
- What if all I had to do is ask for _____?

- It is possible to feel _____.
- I think I can have/feel _____.
- I choose to feel _____ in mind, body, and spirit.
- I would love feeling/being/having _____.
- I chose to broadcast a frequency of _____.
- Show me the next logical step toward feeling/having_____; make it easy, obvious, and fast.
- I allow myself to receive circumstances, people, and situations that bring me the feeling of _____.
- I co-create this feeling with God/source.
- I invite _____to flow in to me from my head to my abdomen, legs, feet, and ground to the earth and back through me in a circuit.
- I am transmitting and receiving the feeling of _____.
- I am in harmony with _____.
- I am in agreement with_____.
- I feel _____now. That is my truth.
- I radiate _____.
- I am worthy of receiving _____.
- I know I can have _____.
  Please bring it to me now.
- The past is over. I can focus on _____ now.
- I am in present time and I am feeling _____.
- I am now programmed to feel _____.
- And so be it, let it be done. Make it so, it will be done from this day forward. Thank you.

Breathe in, grab your wrist, and let out your breath. Take a minute to sense how you feel now.

(Reproducible)

My Goal

A Way to Reprogram You Mind
To a Positive Emotion

Define your **PEP** in terms of a goal. Declaring a goal then attaching emotion from the subconscious mind through the conscious mind using the senses creates a habit and ultimately sympathetic resonance, harmony, and alignment. It adds mass. Most of us ultimately want to feel joy and purpose. We want good health, happiness, or things in our lives, but we don't understand how to manifest them. I believe that we can create something in our lives if we resonate with it at an emotional level. It is just a matter of releasing negative programs and moving through lack or neutrality, and then ultimately using **Positive Emotional Programming.** We must begin to vibrate on the frequency of the emotion of what we desire before we can manifest it. We can do that first with our thoughts and then with our emotions. Remember our transmitter and our emoter?

Think about your goal in life. Maybe you just want to be happy or healthy. Are you hoping for a mate, a new house, to have more money, or to be trim? These are tangible things that we consciously want. We can sense them with our brain. We can manifest them if we broadcast the emotion attached to having them.

Whatever you desire, declare it in positive terms. The more specific you are, the more coherent the frequency. After you declare it, describe what you want with your senses. How would it feel if you had it? The goal is to create it by focusing thought and giving it emotional mass. It is suggested in numerous success books that looking at, feeling, and thinking about your goal when you are in the alpha state can speed up manifestation. The **alpha state** is when your conscious mind is less likely to interfere with your subconscious mind. In other words, you can feel it better without rationalizing as much. That is why we were taught to pray at night or in the morning as well.

You may wish to create a dream board with pictures of your goal. Writing the words in cursive on white paper with blue ink over and over will focus thought and will help you begin to broadcast the emotion you are creating about it. Cursive writing makes thousands of connections in your brain and works well with your transmitter and emoter. Getting your body into physical proximity with your goal is optimal. I suggest doing whatever it takes to give it mass and bring it to realization through all of your senses and to be sure to feel the emotions of having it.

Using your imagination allows the free flow of energy between you and God/source. We are creative beings. We are designed to create and expand. It feels good, and we are living our purpose.

As you do this process, you may find your conscious mind trying to rationalize how to get what you want. When your transmitter rationalizes, you divert the energy away from the emoter. Then, you cannot manifest what you want. **You get what you emote from your heart, not what you think from your brain.**

> *"I never let my schooling interfere with my education."*
>
> —*Zig Ziglar*

Educate *from the Latin word educo, to draw forth from within or to bring out.*

Teach *is an old English word, to point out, to impart knowledge upon.*

Define Your Goal

What does it look, smell, feel, taste, and sound like to have it? Try to describe how it would feel to have it.

_____

_____

_____

_____

_____

_____

_____

_____

_____

_____

_____

_____

_____

_____

_____

_____

_____

_____

_____

_____

_____

_____

_____

_____

_____

Look at this description several times a day. If you find yourself feeling doubt or fear, go back to pages 76-77 to find out what frequency is causing resistance and do the releasing process on pages 78-79. You must release negative frequencies, and then go through the neutral place of lack before you can begin to create the positive frequency.

To start the flow of energy toward your positive program, ask yourself questions such as "What if this were real? What if it could happen? What if it is my truth?" Work yourself up to believing it could happen by repetition every day. Be sure to use your senses as much as possible. Use the list of positive emotions on pages 81-82. If you find yourself not doing it, you are probably rationalizing or trying to figure out how with your brain transmitter The goal is to start with a seed of intention and add mass to it by focusing on it. As you begin to believe it you attach emotion to it, then it becomes reality.

(Reproducible)

Re-Minders

Spaced Repetition and Programming Yourself with PEP

- Repeat the positive process on pages 83-84 with your goal at least twice a day for a minimum of two weeks, preferably in the alpha state.

- As a constant reminder, bless a piece of jewelry or an item that you see, wear, or touch regularly with your goal. That way, every time you are in contact with it, you **re-mind** your subconscious.

- Use note cards or sticky notes with the statements posted everywhere.

- Catch yourself thinking negative thoughts, tell yourself "no," and shift to your new program.

- Instead of worrying about the worst scenario, think about the best scenario.

- "What if" yourself into positive thoughts: "What if it is over, and I am safe?" "What if I do get that job?" "What if I am well?" "What if I was thin?"

- Do some deep breathing. Breathe in the goal and out resistance. You can do this anywhere. Try it as you go to sleep and as you wake up or even in the car.

- Get yourself into an environment where you can sense and feel the positive emotional frequency you are trying to create. You will begin to resonate with it. It becomes a habit and part of you at the thought level because you are living, breathing, tasting, smelling, feeling, and seeing it. Then you begin emoting, intending, and broadcasting it with all of your senses. As this happens, you begin to give it mass and then it begins to manifest at the quantum level.

Gratitude List

One of the most uplifting and powerful things we can do is write **gratitude list** on white paper with blue ink. Writing and thinking about things we appreciate gives those things mass and power. It makes us feel grateful, raises our vibration, and keeps us positive. We will create and manifest more things to make us feel grateful. Gratitude comes from the heart and the subconscious mind. Thankfulness comes from the head and the conscious mind.

It is important to feel gratitude with positive emotions. It allows energy to flow in its natural path. If we feel bad, we broadcast things like worry, doubt, or fear, and our goals cannot be created.

After all the PEP training, consider how powerful writing, expressing, transmitting, and emoting a gratitude list can be. Think about what we can create by the law of attraction when we broadcast the emotional frequency of gratitude.

Try it: What are you grateful for?

_____

_____

_____

_____

_____

_____

_____

_____

_____

_____

_____

_____
_____
_____
_____
_____
_____
_____
_____
_____
_____
_____
_____
_____
_____
_____
_____
_____
_____
_____
_____
_____
_____
_____

Have Faith!

"The substance of things hoped for, the evidence of things not seen."
—Hebrews 11:1

(Reproducible)

Dowsing or Divining

Okay, so here is where science meets spirituality, and frankly it was a shot in the dark for me at first. In my quest to understand the power of words and how all of this frequency stuff works, I was handed a pendulum at a seminar in New York City. I spent time experimenting, learning, and researching divining. It is outside the box thinking that brought me to this concept. It is challenging for many people to grasp this idea.

I started by researching divining for water. The diviner uses thought to transmit the frequency of water to the universe. The diviner begins to resonate with water. At the molecular level, the diviner's body begins to vibrate on the same frequency as water in sympathetic resonance or harmony. It isn't difficult because our body is made up of water, and thoughts travel very quickly. Using a divining rod as an indicator, the diviner finds water because when the rod gets close enough to a source of water, it matches the frequency of the diviner's intention. The diviner's body is the conduit. Some diviners use a silver coin as an amplifier. Divining with a pendulum works the same way. Fortune tellers use a pendulum to focus intention and match frequencies. They can focus thought with intention and translate frequencies into words, some more accurately than others.

I determined that, if water and oxygen are things that can be influenced with focused thought, it should work to dowse for emotions, because a thought is a quantifiable thing, thanks to Dr. Emoto's experiment.

I spent a considerable amount of time learning how to use a pendulum. I stumbled upon two amazing books: *The Pendulum Bridge to Infinite Knowing* and *The Pendulum Charts, Volume 1*, by Dale W. Olson (Crystalline Publishing, Eugene, Oregon). If you want to learn how to dowse, spend some time learning how to use a pendulum with Dale Olson's books. It takes time to learn, but it is time well spent. Dowsing is a method of translating frequencies from the subconscious into words.

When releasing a program that is stuck in the subconscious mind, it is very important to bring it to the conscious mind. Many people have difficulty believing they are broadcasting certain subconscious frequencies because their conscious mind cannot rationalize it with the senses. In that situation, people cannot always find the emotion with intuition, but a pendulum appears to work.

I talked with a woman who could not manifest money no matter what she tried. I asked her about her childhood and money. She said money was never an issue as a child. So I used the pendulum to find out what frequency she was broadcasting when she thought about money. She was broadcasting guilt. When I told her that, she said, "I don't feel guilty at all." But after thinking about it for a minute, she brought the emotions from the subconscious to the conscious mind. She linked those emotions all the way back in a chain of events to her birth. She was adopted. Her guilt started at pre-birth. She started her life with a need for acceptance. After releasing the emotions of guilt and neediness, and resetting her subconscious program to self-worth, she had a big shift in her energy when she finally accessed that emotional program in her subconscious mind. Her guilt stopped her from accepting money. I would not have been able to access that emotion so easily without the pendulum. That is the gift of divining.

Think about the word divining. Are we connecting with divine energy?

Finding Negative Emotional Programs With a Pendulum

After training yourself to use a pendulum, focus on your condition, belief, or emotion. Use The Pendulum Charts Volume 1 for everything on this page. Hold the pendulum over the yin and yang on page 1, the Master Chart of Dale Olson's pendulum charts.

Ask:
"What am I broadcasting? What is this? What is this? What is this?"
Wait for the pendulum to move to identify the chart number.
Go to the chart that it is pointing to.

Ask:
"What frequency am I broadcasting? What is this? What is this? What is this?"
Watch the pendulum swing over the answer and get your reading.
Go to page 2, The Yes, No Chart of Dale Olson's charts for a yes/no response.

Ask:
"Is there an emotion attached?" Wait for a yes/no response.
If "**yes**", go to chart 38, What Is Going On Chart or chart 50, Alphabet Numerical Chart and ask, "What emotion am I broadcasting?"
If "**no**", then ask, "Is there a belief attached to it?"
If "**yes**", go to chart 39, What Am I Telling Myself Chart or chart 50 and ask, "What is the belief?"

As your accuracy improves, you can just go to chart 50 and have the words spelled out.

Once you have identified the emotion or belief you are broadcasting, you can begin the process of releasing it from your energetic, magnetic field known as your mind.

Chart 1 is where you start.
Chart 2 is a yes/no response.
Chart 38 gives some possible emotions.
Chart 39 gives some possible beliefs.
Chart 37 and chart 42 offer some positive emotions.
Chart 50 will help you spell words.

You can also use the pendulum without Dale's book and just look for yes/no responses as you go through the lists of emotions on pages 76-77 and 81-82 in this book. Yes is vertical, no is horizontal.

(Reproducible)

Glossary

abundance: an ample quantity; affluence, wealth; degree of plentifulness.

Acupressure: the application of pressure with a thumb or fingertip on a specific body part for therapeutic effects.

agreement: harmony of opinion, action, or feeling; a pleasing combination of elements in an arrangement or course of action.

alpha state: the state of relaxation and peaceful awakeness; a condition of being in a stage of growth, changing form, or developing awareness in the conscious mind.

biophotons: a growing body of molecular research that indicates that molecules emit energy and absorb photons.

blockage: the state of being obstructed, blocked, or closed up; hindering the passage, flow, or intended path of energy.

body: a group of organs, fluids, and systems that come together within a human being or animal.

broadcast: to transmit a signal or wave of resonance; to send out a communication to a wide area.

catalyst: a person or thing that causes change.

chords: a segment of line joining an emotion to other recorded levels of consciousness on your time track: the mind records pictures, sound tones vibrations, and emotion simultaneously with chords of association to earlier similar ones.

co-create: to jointly cause to exist: with more than just oneself you are bringing into being, producing, giving rise to a result or creation.

cognition: that which comes to be known through perception, reasoning, or intuition; knowledge.

coherent: marked by orderly, logical, and aesthetically consistent relation of parts.

coherent light: light of one color, monochromatic, and most common source of light for laser.

consciousness: the wide range of mental activities that include sensation, cognition, and conscious thought; our five senses of sight, hearing, smell, taste, and smell.

congestion: to overfill or overcrowd; the accumulation of energy that is not moving fluidly in, on, or around the body.

congruence: the state of being in agreement, harmony, conformity, or correspondence. Two people can easily be in harmonic correspondence.

conversely: reversed, as in position, order, or action, to the contrary, opposite in direction.

counterclockwise: rotating in a circular direction from right to left when seen from the front or above.

disease: disagreement within the body; a state of hardship, difficulty, and effort manifesting in the body; the opposite of being comfortable and free from pain, worry, or agitation.

divine: to know by intuition, inspiration, or reflection.

diviner: a person skilled in using a diving rod or pendulum to discern or sense electric and magnetic energy.

dowsing: the use of a pendulum (plum-bob) of crystal, metal, or other material suspended on a chain. The crystal plum bob is dangled and the user "trains" the responses with his subconscious mind. Generally horizontal movement is "no." Vertical movement is "yes." It is generally believed that the pendulum is trained to move by energy from the subconscious mind of the diviner.

dysfunction: impaired, difficult, painful, or faulty characteristic of a person's body.

EFT: emotional freedom technique, an acupressure technique that includes tapping with one's own fingertips on specific meridian points of the body.

electron: a particle of energy with a negative charge that is a fundamental particle of matter.

emoter: a term created to explain the relationship between the heart and the subconscious mind.

empower: to supply with ability.

energy spectrum: the distribution of energy among a large observable group of waves of energy that function on frequency. The electromagnetic spectrum covers a wide range of wavelengths and photon energies.

flashback: vivid recollection of an experience that took place before present time.

frequency: the number of occurrences of a repeating event per unit time. The measurement of wavelengths on the energy/light/radio wave spectrum is accomplished by calculating the number of times that cycle occurs within a specific time interval; can be accomplished as a sine wave.

gamma rays: high frequency (very short wavelengths) of electromagnetic radiation, produced by subatomic particle interactions.

genetically related programs, beliefs, or imprints: energetic marks or outlines, circuited into your mind/body that have been blueprinted and downloaded from ancestors.

hooks in, on, and around the body: fasteners, energy connections, the point where a negative energy chord is connected, creating a circuit to a memory.

intention: the specific purpose in doing, the end or goal that is aimed.

interference: anything that alters, modifies, or disrupts a message as it travels along a channel between a source and a receiver.

intuition: understanding without apparent effort. The mind perceives the agreement or disagreement with thoughts or ideas.

invoke: bring to mind.

Isaac Newton: (1643–1727) English physicist, mathematician, astronomer, philosopher, alchemist, and theologian considered by many scholars to be one of the most influential people in recorded human history.

karate chop point: outside edge of the hand near the point of the pinkie joint; the group of muscles running between the wrist and the first joint on the smallest finger on the outside edge of one's hand.

karma: the concept where actions or deeds cause a cycle of cause and effect; deeds viewed as actively shaping past, present, and future experiences.

Law of Attraction: basically, like attracts like; the idea that intense positive or negative thoughts and emotions attract like similar energy in the form of more experiences, circumstances, and people with matching emotional frequencies.

lepton: an elementary particle found in atoms directly tied to chemical properties.

magnetic field: a field of force produced by moving electric charges that vary in time.

mastermind: a person (or group of synchronized people) who originate the energy for directing and creating intelligence.

mind: interpreted as the collective aspects of intellect, consciousness, and intelligence; the conscious mental events an individual feels, perceives, wills, and reasons.

molecule: an electrically neutral group of at least two atoms held together by covalent chemical bonds.

muscle testing, applied kinesiology: a method of evaluating the body's response when slight pressure is applied to a large muscle group; the practice of locating information on energy blockages. (full explanation is presented on goodhealthinfo.net.)

negative attachments: negativities that have become part of your reactive mind. They produce thoughts and emotions in us that feel like they are coming from us, but in truth, are like a recording or program.

neutron: a subatomic particle with no net electric charge; a part of an atom.

pathogen: an infectious agent such as a virus, bacteria, or fungus that can cause disease.

pathway: the intended path or "road" for travel; a connection between neural receptors, via nerves to and from the brain and or mind.

pendulum: a weight suspended from a pivot on a string or chain, so it can swing freely. When the weight is displaced from its resting equilibrium position, it is subject to swing until the restoring force of gravity brings it back to stationary equilibrium. In dowsing, electromagnetic force displaces the weight from the equilibrium position. When the discerned electromagnetism is dispersed, the weight will slow and stop its swing and return to equilibrium.

phonetic sound: the sounds of speech; the physical properties of speech, sound, and the physiological production, acoustic properties, auditory perception, and effect on the nerves of the receiver.

present time: the concept of current time; now, this moment or period of time as perceived and distinguished from past and future.

proactive: acting in advance to deal with an expected event in the future.

program: a set of coded instructions that enables a machine to perform; instructions in our mind that have the body perform or react without engaging the conscious awareness.

proton: a stable, positively charged part of an atom.

Qi Gong: a Chinese system of breathing exercises, body postures and movements, and mental concentration, intended to maintain good health and control the flow of vital energy.

quantifiable: to determine or express the quantity of.

Quantum Energetic Coaching (QEC) : a method of coaching people to understand the relationship between energy and emotion in the body and mind; developed by Donna Scott-Nusrala.

quantum energy: an elemental unit of energy.

quantum physics: a branch of physics that deals with the particle and wave behavior and interactions of energy and matter.

quark: an elementary part of an electron.

radiate: to send out waves; to emit from a center in a glowing manner.

reality: the state of things as they are, as they exist, rather than as they may appear or may be thought to be.

realm: a community or kingdom of sovereignty.

receiver: a device that converts a radio signal from a modulated wave into usable audio or video information.

Reiki: a technique developed by a Japanese Buddhist in which healing energy is transferred in the palms of hands.

re-mind: to cause someone to remember something; to improve clarity or recall in your mind.

rerouting: to send along a different route; to remove a circuit and route the thought process through new neuron pathways.

reset: to clear pending errors or events and bring a system to a normal condition or initial state.

resistance: a measure of the degree to which a pathway of flow opposes an electric current flowing smoothly through it; the force that opposes motion.

resonate: a phenomenon, which occurs with all types of vibrations or waves. Balanced resonance occurs when a system is able to easily transfer energy between two or more modes, such a kinetic energy and potential energy.

self-sabotage: the unconscious deliberate action aimed at weakening self through obstruction or disruption, causing change in direction.

source: the start, beginning, origin point. The source of life can be contemplated as the beginning point for frequency, tone, and vibration.

spectrum: the image of visible light that is discerned as color according to wavelength when white light is dispersed through a prism.

spin clockwise: a circular movement that proceeds from the top to the right then down and then to the left and back to the top in the motion of the hands of a clock.

spirit: the vital energy of a being.

sympathetic resonance: a phenomenon wherein a passive vibratory body responds to external vibrations of harmonic likeness. An opera singer who breaks a glass with her voice is singing in sympathetic resonance.

subconscious mind: thoughts that are not consciously acknowledged, yet have force and effect. The genetic or energetic blueprint that has fight or flight ready without the mind having to pause and access the memory to create an environment or reaction that is appropriate for survival.

tapping: the use of rhythmic finger tip contact with specific acupressure points on the body to stimulate the energetic meridians.

The Word: the title assigned to sacred written words, and most often referring to the Old/New Testament.

third eye: a symbol of enlightenment. It is also considered an EFT tapping point between the eyebrows. It is associated with direct perceptions, intuition, imagination, visualization, concentration, self-mastery, and the pineal gland.

timeline: a scale of time from a person's beginning that can be graphed and marked with significant moments.

tone: the pitch, high or low sound.

transmitter: an electronic device that produces and broadcasts energy.

transmute: the conversion of negative electromagnetic energy frequencies to positive energy frequencies.

vibration: to oscillate periodically; a periodic motion of particles in alternately opposite directions from the equilibrium.

visualize: representation of information or knowledge activating imagination.

yin and yang: a Chinese symbol used to describe positive and negative forces.

Yoga: a meditative practice with mental, verbal, and physical ritual.

Suggested Reading

Byrne Rhonda, The Secret. Beyond Words, 2006.

Hawkins, David R., Power vs. Force. Hay House 2002.

Hicks, Jerry and Ester, Ask and It Is Given. Hay House 2004.

Hill, Napoleon, Outwitting the Devil. Sterling, 2012.

Hill, Napoleon, The Law of Success in 16 Lessons. Wilshire Books, 2000, Napoleon Hill 1938.

References and Special Thanks

Callahan, Dr. Roger: developer of Thought Field Therapy (TFT), the origin of meridian tapping therapy that uses acupressure techniques to balance the body's energy system. www.rogercallahan.com.

Emoto, Dr. Masaru: Japanese author best known for energy research and studies of the human consciousness. His books generally focus on the properties and healing power of water. Water, Consciousness and Intent, Dr. Masaru Emoto, YouTube. www.masaru-emoto.net/english/

Hill, Napoleon: American author who wrote successful books, including Think and Grow Rich and The Law of Success in Sixteen Lessons, influenced by Andrew Carnegie.

Ji, Sayer: author and lecturer promoting natural and integrative healing, wellness, and health therapies, Sayer Ji, "Biophotons: The Human Body Emits, Communicates With, and is Made From Light," GreenMedInfo.com, June 2013.

Olson, Dale W.: author, The Bridge to Infinite Knowing and The Pendulum Charts, Volume 1 and Volume 2, Dale W. Olson, Crystalline Publishing 2009 Website: www.getintuitive.com.

Ortner, Jessica, Nick, and Alex: authors, speakers, siblings and producers of the documentary film "The Tapping Solution," which demonstrates the process of emotional freedom technique. The Tapping Solution, www.thetappingsolution.com.

*For more information about Quantum Energetic Coaching
or to schedule a private session in person or over the phone,
speaking engagement, or group session with Donna, please
visit the energyofemotion.com or at www.amopublishing.com,
contact donna@amopublishing.com or call 440-554-7505.*

Look for Donna Scott-Nusrala on Facebook, Twitter and Linkedin